# RareVisions
## & Roadside Revelations

by Randy Mason, Michael Murphy and Don Mayberger
Hosts of KCPT's Award-Winning Travel Series

PUBLIC TELEVISION 19 · DIGITAL 18

Rare Visions and Roadside Revelations
By Randy Mason, Michael Murphy and Don Mayberger

Edited by Doug Worgul
Book design and production by Kelly Ludwig
Production coordination by Angee Simmons

Published by KANSAS CITY STAR BOOKS
1729 Grand Boulevard
Kansas City, Missouri, USA 64108
All rights reserved
Copyright © 2002 The Kansas City Star
★ KANSAS CITY STAR BOOKS

FIRST EDITION
Library of Congress Control Number: 2001094887
ISBN: 0-9712920-2-7

Printed in the United States of America
By Walsworth Publishing Co.
To order copies call StarInfo, (816) 234-4636
For more information about this and other fine books from Star Books visit our Web site at www.kcstar.com or visit www.starbookspreview.com.

# thanks

So many people have helped make the television show that makes this book possible, including our KCPT production team — Mark Stamm, Carol Sherman, Clayton Stubbs, Richard Carr, Jeff Evans, Jeff Hudson, Angee Simmons, Sandy Woodson, Cynthia Smith, Dave Welsh, and "the big guy" KCPT President Bill Reed.

Thanks also to our musical contributors, Kelly Werts and the Plaid Family, as well as our friends in the folk art community like Ken & Kate Anderson, John Hachmeister, Ray Wilber, Lisa Stone, Bill Swislow, Ted Degener, Roger Manley, The Orange Show Foundation and Larry Harris, who saved our tail with so many good photos.

Kudos to our cohorts at the Kansas City Star book division, senior editor Doug Worgul and publisher, Doug Weaver. But our most heartfelt thanks go to designer Kelly Ludwig and our own Angee Simmons for their unrelenting dedication to making this look as good as possible.

Due to space limitations in this book, we haven't been able to feature all the people and places we've seen in our travels. But in the back, you can find bonus listings and directions to more artists and attractions that we heartily recommend.

# map o' contents

On the course of editing this book, I was reminded over and over again of the old adage about the bumblebee. You know the one. It seems physicists long ago determined that bumblebees can't actually fly. Apparently, their wings aren't big enough in proportion to their bodies and so the mechanics for flight are all wrong. However, because bumblebees don't really understand the laws of physics, they just go ahead and fly anyway.

The artists documented in the KCPT television program "Rare Visions & Roadside Revelations" are a lot like bumblebees. They don't possess the education or training to create art, but most of them don't know that, or don't care. So they just go right ahead and make art anyway. And the art they make enlightens, entertains, disturbs, and liberates. Because that is what art does.

KCPT 's Randy Mason, Mike Murphy, and Don Mayberger, the creators of "Rare Visions & Roadside Revelations," have done us all a great service. In their lighthearted quest to discover and document America's folk artists and visionaries and in their wholehearted enthusiasm for both the journey and its destinations, they have shown us that great art is not a product of an artist's degrees but of an artist's heart.

This book is not a printed version of the television program. Rather, it is a viewers' companion. It is the collected reflections of Messrs. Mason, Murphy, and Mayberger, their memories and observations. Consider it a big ol' postcard from the road, or a gift shop souvenir. And while it's not necessarily a travel guide, if it inspires readers to jump in the car with the kids and a camera, well, that's just fine.

Readers will find that this book tends to ramble and meander a bit. Like the program itself. But there are signposts along the way. At the beginning of each chapter you'll find a Polaroid photograph of either Randy or Mike indicating who wrote that particular chapter. And then you'll find occasional sidebars written by Don, The Camera Guy. Cleverly, these are indicated by a cute little camera icon.

So, sit back and enjoy this freewheeling journey of discovery. Perhaps it will stir something inside your soul. Before you know it you may be building a monument to a saint or a dead rock star in your own backyard, using bottlecaps and bubblegum.

-Doug Worgul,
Editor
Kansas City, 2002

welcome to

~~This~~ is a show
About things you can see
Witnout goin' far
~~And often for free~~
~~And a lot of 'em are free~~
~~It's not always pretty~~
~~Three guys in a van~~
~~Nothing more to guide 'em~~
~~Than a bare-boned plan~~

If you thaght there was
nothing
In the ~~great~~ midwest old Heartland
~~You haven't~~ ~~hit the highway~~
~~hit these~~ far caught
~~Hit the blacktop~~
~~these guys in the van~~

Look out
They're drivin' hard
Checkin' out art in their own backyard

Randy does the steerin'
So he won't hurl
Mike's got the maps
A real man of the world

That's Don with the camera
Gets kinda heavy on his shoulder
And their giant ball o' tape
Is a world-record-holder

Look out
They're drivim' hard
Checkin' out life in their own backyard

Original lyrics to Rare Visions theme song
written by Kelly Werts and Randy Mason.

Coffee stains courtesy of Randy Mason

125 East Thirty-First Street    Kansas City, Missouri 64108

# "RANDY DOES THE STEERING, SO HE WON'T HURL."

ot the most lyrical of lyrics, but alas, it's true. Those demons of motion sickness that ruthlessly ruled my childhood travels (just ask my parents) settle right down if I'm allowed to drive. So drive I do.

Of course, some might say it's also a great way to rationalize claiming the "power seat", where a coffee-fueled producer can easily exert the kinds of "control" on which he thrives. But hey, that's enough pop psychology.

The real question is "Just how is it that I got to go ride around the country exploring the quirkier side of our culture anyway?"

Well, I guess there are a few resume-type reasons. I actually did get a degree in journalism from KU, and have been making TV features about the arts for nearly twenty years. My small-town background comes in handy too...but the truth is I DON'T HAVE A CLUE!

Back in 1995, when we set out to do a show about our favorite art and oddities in Kansas, that's really all we had in mind. One show. For reasons we still can't explain, something about "three guys in a van" clicked with viewers. The response was so favorable that our wise and perceptive bosses at KCPT suggested it might behoove us to make a few more shows. Now thirty shows and twenty-five states later, we're still clueless and still having fun. And I hope we'll keep making more.

As long as I get to drive.

Randy

## "MIKE'S GOT THE MAPS, SUCH A MAN OF THE WORLD"

Though you can usually find me in the front passenger seat with a map on my lap (when I'm not sleeping!), I'm not sure where this line really came from. I'd like to think that I've been recognized as the guy who does most of the navigating on our little show, getting us from point A to point B in the shortest possible time, but let's face the truth — even though I've been lucky enough to see very small parts of five very large continents, that "man of the world" thing only shows up because 'world' sort of rhymes with "hurl," and that's what Randy does if he doesn't drive!

I like to tell people who ask about the show that we're just out on the road, stopping at all the places your father would never stop when you were a kid. Did that sign say "World's largest something or other, just 2 miles ahead?" Or "Two- headed cow, next exit?" These are signs I can't drive past.

And I love the art. There's always a story behind every place we stop and I really like finding that story. When you stumble on a man making his own tribute to the Trail of Tears, or a woman like L.V. Hull painting shoes to adorn her front yard, and you see the depth of commitment, the drive, the love for what they do, it's like finding buried treasure. My life is better for the people I meet, and that's the bottom line.

Did I do anything to deserve this good fortune? Probably not. I grew up on the outskirts of Kansas City, in a small town called Parkville, where my childhood was pretty nondescript, and eventually I earned a degree in communications from the University of Missouri at Kansas City, which in all sincerity qualifies me for nothing. But I've been lucky enough to practice this television trade at KCPT for more than 20 years, and I've learned a few tricks along the way. And just as soon as I remember those tricks I'm going to put them in a show, I promise....

*Mike*

# "THERE'S DON WITH THE CAMERA, KINDA HEAVY ON HIS SHOULDER."

And he just can't seem to keep quiet. Who ever heard of a talking cameraman anyway? I just want to say up front that I never intended to be a talking Camera Guy. So then, how did I land this nice-work-if-you-can-get-it job, in which I get to go to amazing places and meet fascinating people, you might ask? It just could be some twisted form of justice.

I was born in Detroit a half century ago, the second of seven boys. There may have been some kind of state law at the time that prevented the transporting of more than six boys across state lines for the purpose of recreation. Or it could be that my folks were just working too hard to go anywhere. The net effect was that when I was a kid, family road trips were few and far between. So when I got the chance back in 1995 to hit the road with Randy and Mike with the vague purpose of making television, I willingly jumped in the back of that Chrysler minivan, and I've been there ever since. I just couldn't keep the kid in me bottled up, and before I knew it, I was the narrator. And to all the nice people who tell me that I'm fortunate to be doing what I'm doing and ask if they could please come along, I'd have to say you're right about the luck part, but unfortunately those Chrysler minivans aren't getting any bigger.

P.S. What's up with us playing catch? Well, it started as a way to stretch out and unwind off camera. Then one day, I just kept rolling, and (as so many things do) it ended up in the show.... Now, regardless of whether you like it or hate it, it's something we make a point of doing every time out.

Don CG

Nokona, the "Best Boy"

# Hiawatha, Ks. to Lucas, Ks.

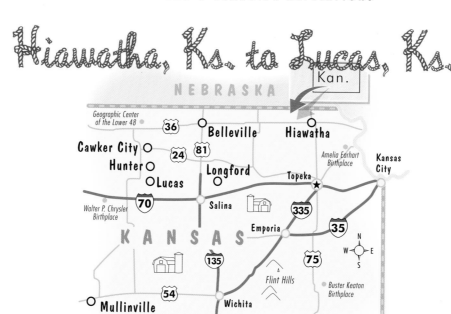

NEBRASKA

Kan.

Geographic Center of the Lower 48

36  Belleville  Hiawatha

Cawker City  24  81

Hunter  Longford

O Lucas  Amelia Earhart Birthplace  Kansas City

Topeka

Walter P. Chrysler Birthplace  Salina  335

K A N S A S  Emporia  35

N
W  E
S

135  75

Flint Hills  Buster Keaton Birthplace

54

O Mullinville  Wichita

Randy

## KANSAS IS COOL

've known all along that the ol' "Home on the Range" is a hip state, even though as a native, I've done my share of complaining about it. And when it comes to offbeat art and strange creations in unexpected places, the Sunflower State more than holds its own.

Take the Davis Memorial in Hiawatha, for example. No, it wasn't made by a Kansan, it just has a great story. You see, after a lifetime of feeling snubbed by his wife's family, old Mr. Davis chose to have an incredibly ornate gravesite made, just so there wouldn't be any money left for them to inherit! And it's a story told in stone, a pictorial history of he and his wife at various stages in their marriage, culminating in the sad, mysterious Vacant Chair.

## WHERE THE BUFFALO ROAM

T hen there's Ray O. Smith's Concretealo near Longford, Kansas. Ray O. could be a little crusty, it's true. I know he sure got tired of trying to explain to me how big a "section" is (OK, it's a square, a mile long on each side, I finally got it!).  But man, that giant buffalo he built overlooking the Flint Hills was truly something to behold. In back of his house, he'd also put up a massive rock wall and a huge stone map of the U.S., using rocks he'd gathered from every state.

Ray O. told us when his time came he didn't want to be buried in the cemetery because "it was full of dead people." He'd prefer being laid to rest under the buffalo. When we heard of his passing, we were happy to learn that his wish came true.

## SPIN CYCLE

ver in Belleville, Kansas, not far from the Nebraska border, the Boyer Gallery is another testimonial to how much a man can do in spite of adversity. Paul Boyer lost his legs in an accident in 1966, but hasn't let that keep him from using his hands to create one amazing mechanical marvel after another. Rube Goldberg style creations where ball bearings bounce around, gears and gizmos whirl and turn, chickens shoot baskets with their tails, and an Indian tribe partys hearty. Some of them are corny, some profoundly beautiful, and they're all made from scrap parts and old appliance motors.

Paul's a shy man, who for years brought these things to the county fair just because he loved to see people's reactions from afar. I'm sure he likes what he sees, since you can't stay here long without cracking a smile. A really big smile.

Of course, we managed to leave the gallery smiling so much that we forgot an important piece of TV equipment, which we had to backtrack 20 miles to retrieve. Thankfully the Boyers waited around for us. I guess we were just in too big a hurry to get back to Cawker City, Kansas, which you may realize is a Very Important Place to us. It's where the World's Largest Ball of Twine sits in its own gazebo right on US-24. It's where the light bulb (if that's what you want to call it) went on for our own Big Ball of Videotape.

# KNOT SO FAST

awker City's claim to fame started with a man named Frank Stoeber, who was tired of all those loose strands getting in his way, so he did something about it. He started winding and never looked back. That was in the 50s. And in the 80s, when some other towns (like Darwin, Minnesota) started making claims about their Big Balls, the city responded by starting an annual twine-a-thon to keep the record at home. It worked. Strangely enough, while we were doing a brief interpretive dance around the ball who should drive by but one of Frank's grandsons. Are we lucky or what?

Don & Randy with John Stoeber, Frank Stoeber's grandson

## SONGBIRD OF THE PLAINS

or decades now, one place to test your luck in these parts has been , Vera's Tavern in Hunter, Kansas. There's not much else in Hunter, and not all that much you'd call special about this small, dimly lit building with its mismatched furniture and tractor seat barstools. The difference here is and always has been Vera herself.

Sooner or later, every night she'd turn off the jukebox, perhaps even climb up on a pool table, and belt out "The Wings of a Dove." And the crowd would go crazy. Vera also likes to dance a bit, though I regret twirling her a little further than her shoulder really wanted to go. I also regret those things we wrote about Tom Brokaw on the ceiling.

## BACK TO THE GARDEN

And then, there's Lucas, which may be the Center of The Universe for grassroots art lovers. For starters, this tiny north central Kansas town is home to the Garden of Eden. Not the one in the Bible, the one old S.P. Dinsmoor poured forth in his back yard with that miracle compound of its day (the late 1800s)--concrete! Dinsmoor was a Civil War veteran and one of those Kansas populists who liked to ruffle the status quo. He also just happened to have an amazing eye for sculpting, a passion he didn't even indulge until he was in his sixties.

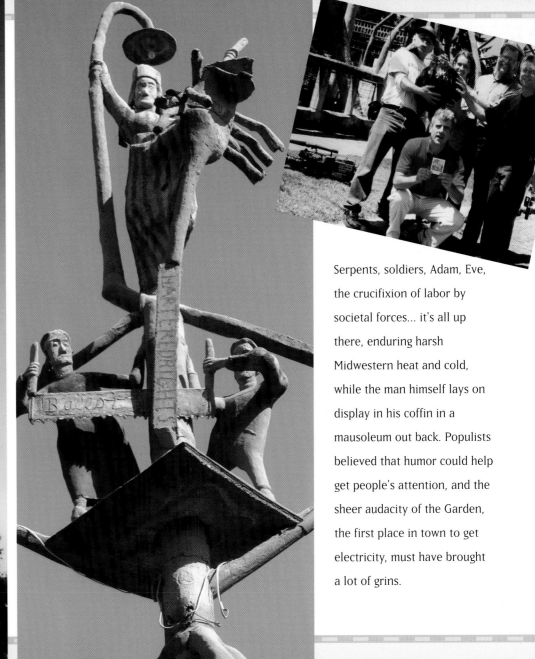

Serpents, soldiers, Adam, Eve, the crucifixion of labor by societal forces... it's all up there, enduring harsh Midwestern heat and cold, while the man himself lays on display in his coffin in a mausoleum out back. Populists believed that humor could help get people's attention, and the sheer audacity of the Garden, the first place in town to get electricity, must have brought a lot of grins.

But the town wasn't always crazy about it. At one point, there was serious talk of bulldozing the Garden down. Luckily, cooler heads prevailed. And Dinsmoor's vision (or something in the water!) seemed to have rubbed off on more than a few others. For example, just around the corner, a schoolteacher named Florence Deeble built a mini-Mt. Rushmore in her yard and other sculptural re-creations of places she'd vacationed. She did it, as she told us one afternoon while sitting on her front porch, because she "just loved rocks."

Leroy Wilson in nearby Luray apparently loved paint, since he covered every square inch of his basement, repeatedly, in psychedelic swirls. And out by Wilson Lake, a farmer named Ed Root sculpted dozens, if not hundreds, of whimsically massive monuments made from concrete and kitchenware.

Thankfully, Ed's sculptures were hauled away years ago, just before the new reservoir inundated the place. They ended up eventually (along with parts of Wilson's bathroom) in downtown Lucas at the Grassroots Art Center.

This place has it all, including our videos, for which we're eternally grateful. But seriously, curator Rosslyn Schultz has done an amazing job here. She's given a home to the Inez Marshall collection, large limestone pieces from a lady who carved houses and cars and stone guitars just down the road in Portis at her Continental Sculpture Hall.

And the place just keeps growing. Rosslyn's even grabbed a few of M.T. Liggett's provocative (some would say provoking) signs you may have seen next to Highway 54 in Mullinville, Kansas. There they run the length of a football field, spinning in the wind and railing about the peccadilloes of local and national politics.

But best of all, she's found a place to display Herman Divers' pull-tab motorcycle. He built it in Topeka, using nothing but those little metal rings pulled from pop and beer cans in days of yore. Herman knew he could use them to make things, like a hat, a coat, an umbrella and a rug. "I don't know how I knew, I just did," he told us. But the full-size motorcycle, with its wheels that actually turn, is the pull-tab *piece de resistance*. And all the proof I need that Kansans are darned clever people! — *RM*

# Norborne, Mo. to Audobon, Ia.

*Mike*

## HAMMER ON

Sometimes there's nothing quite so lovely as obsession. A guy starts collecting something as mundane and everyday as hammers, hooks his wife into the same dream, and before you know it, he's got to put up a building next to his house just to have some place to put the darn things.

More than 2,700 of 'em at last count, and still counting. And we're not talking about 2,700 plain old ordinary everyday hammers. Oh no, these are 2,700 different, unique, individual, no two-the-same hammers. I'm talking about a load of hammers approaching the line between sanity and not. And Glen and Judy Albrecht know about each and every one of em', because they've all got stories. With a smile and a laugh,

and warmth that made us feel like family, these folks can talk your ear off about hammers.

Norborne, Missouri, where the Albrechts live, looks like a normal enough town. Kids play in tidy front yards, people know their neighbors, and the water seems safe to drink. But something infected Glen and Judy with the hammer bug, and there's no known cure for that ailment. You can only hope to treat the symptoms, and for the Albrechts, that only means one thing.

More hammers!

## IN IOWA WE FOUND A MOUNTAIN

The 8th wonder of the world is in Iowa. At least, that's what the advertisements say, and who am I to argue with them. Rising out of the small town of West Bend (Pop. 862), in a part of Iowa where the landscape is seldom disturbed by anything larger than a grain silo, lies the Grotto of the Redemption. Grottos are a phenomenon we've seen a lot of over the years, but this one is King of the Hill.

Father Paul Dobberstein, creator of the grotto, was born in Germany in 1872 and immigrated to America in 1893. As the story goes, while a student at St. Francis Seminary he became seriously ill with pneumonia and promised to honor the Blessed Virgin should he recover his health. And apparently, when Dobberstein made a promise, he kept it, in a big way!

Assigned to the West Bend parish in 1898, by 1901 he was digging the footings for his grotto. He worked with rock, minerals, crystals and concrete, hauling materials by the train carload. Apparently, Father Paul had studied geology during his student years, and prized working with the finest minerals. He had an assistant named Matt Szerensce, and the two gathered materials relentlessly, sometimes hitching rides with their railroad hand car from passing trains, traveling to far off places to bring home another load of interesting stone or minerals.

And they built, and built, and built. Pathways wind in and around the grounds, leading one through a maze of religious riches. In the grotto, the story of the Redemption, caves honoring the Blessed Mother, the 12 Stations of the Cross, and on and on, are all woven together in a tapestry of gilded stone.

Dobberstein built other remarkable things throughout the region as well. In Humbolt, he was commissioned to build a fountain to honor the memory of a young girl who died of tuberculosis. South of West Bend he erected a memorial to those who fought in W.W.II. Built in what was once the town of Old Rolfe, it now lies basically in the middle of nowhere, the town having moved some years ago. In Dubuque, Iowa, he created the Holy Family Grotto. And in La Crosse, Wisconsin, he built the Saint Rose Grotto, his last, which is dedicated to his sister and two nieces, who were both members of the Franciscan Sisters of Perpetual Adoration.

Considering the sheer quantity of work, I figure Father Dobberstein must have lived about 150 years. But of course, he didn't. He'd just been a man with a calling, a man on a mission, and he'd had a promise to keep. He died in 1954, leaving behind 42 years of dedication and commitment, a richness of spirit that continues to inspire those lucky enough to find their way to what might *really* be the 8th Wonder of the World, in West Bend, Iowa.

*Big time thanks to Lisa Stone and her awesome book*
Sacred Spaces and Other Places *for info and insights.*

# BULL TO SPARE

Every town wants to be home to a "world's biggest" something or other. At least, it seems that way when we're out there on the road. And we're not immune to this syndrome, either. After all, we are traveling with the world's largest ball of videotape. In Audubon, Iowa, Albert the Bull "steaks" his claim to "world's largest." And all I can say is I've never seen a bigger bull.    — MM

All I can say is we skipped a meal that probably would have been edible in the restaurant rich city of Omaha to go find Albert the Bull before dark. Now Albert may indeed be big, but as a vegetarian heading into the hinterlands of Iowa to go look for him was, in my opinion, one of the World's Largest Mis-steaks.
*Don CG*

ALBERT THE BULL
AUDUBON IOWA • 50025

# Sedalia, Mo. to St. Louis, Mo.

Randy

## P B & H ?

Peanut butter slathered on a hamburger patty. It's called a guberburger. And The Wheel Drive-In has been cookin' 'em up for decades, ever since a traveling salesman traded the owner the recipe. Folks around Sedalia love them. Some are known to drive long distances to partake in this local food tradition. The preferred manner of partaking is to pile all your regular burger toppings atop the peanut butter. It's an acquired taste.

If location is one of the elements of successful business, the Wheel Drive-In's got it with a capital "L". It sits at the busiest intersection in town, where lake-bound traffic passes by. Its dècor is retro without pretense and even if you don't want anything "guber," it's fun to belly up to the horseshoe shaped counter and enjoy the kind of ambience no franchise operation will ever have.

Now, Don says, if they'd just develop a Garden Guberburger...

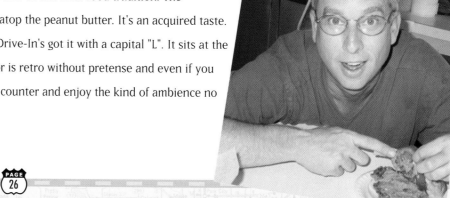

## LORD OF THE TICKS

**m**ike Robins spent much of his youth in Indonesia (where there are probably very few burger joints to choose from) soaking up sights and sounds that now contribute exotic flavor to his lovely little farmstead outside Ashland. The masks Mike makes on his farm seem out of place in mid-Missouri, stone images mounted on trees and attached to the sides of his house. They peek out of the shrubs and gardens he's meticulously maintained. Some of the masks are painted in bright day-glo colors, others are earth-toned and neutral.

This Tolkien-tinged world that Robins has created is nowhere near a main road. Few will ever see it without an invitation. It's a prime example of how the artistic spirit moves some people to work incredibly hard for incredibly little financial reward.

It's also a great place to get covered with ticks.

## TERMINALLY CREATIVE

By the time you get down around Rolla, Missouri, you know for sure you're in the Ozarks. The roads get windier, the woods denser. And there are caves around most every corner. Such as the Onyx Mountain Caverns, which I think should get honorable mention for its low-key marketing strategy. This family run "non-corporate cave" is tucked into a beautiful, unspoiled hillside. It's not big enough for Jeeps to rumble through, but you can still see plenty of strange formations before heading up to the gift shop to drop a few guilt-free bucks.

Larry Baggett is the one who recommended the cave to us. Larry lives between Newburg and Jerome, just off I-44, along an old stretch of Route 66. When Larry talks, you can't help but listen. "My doctor gave me three years to live twenty years ago" is one of the first things this unpretentious, overall-clad character told us about himself. But it doesn't take long to see that Larry is one sharp guy, with a sharp eye for sculptural form. There's the elegant stone archway over his drive, a tribute to lives lost on the tragic Trail of Tears, which actually passed right over this piece of land.

There are long terraced gardens cascading down the steep hill that is his front yard, sprawling rock walls that a man his age (he started all this in his 6os) should not have been able to do. And there's his colorful, industrial size homemade hot tub out front which has recreational opportunity written all over it!

Then there's Larry's workout rig, where instead of pumping iron, he benches and squats giant rocks that much younger guys on TV can hardly budge. I'm still not sure how to explain Larry's recovery from kidney disease. He says its has something to do with a special diet and a lot of faith. But in the time he was supposed to be dying, he's managed to do more than most of us will in an entire lifetime.

## HE DID IT HIS WAY

Yﾟou've seen it. There on I-70 at the Wright City exit. It's
The King himself, looming large over a little café. But
this is not your ordinary roadside Elvis tribute. It is, as the sign says,
The Elvis Is Alive Museum.

Bill Beeny, the museum's founder and, uh,
curator, is a real estate agent who's been
known to do some Elvis impersonating from
time to time. But that's not really Beeny's main
mission in life. Along with expected photos

and album covers and bits
of goofy Presleyana on
display in his museum,
Beeny bravely dares
expose the truth about
how Elvis' death was
faked!

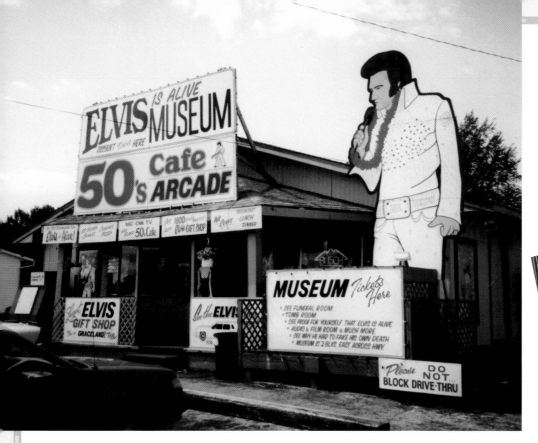

I have driven this stretch of Interstate 70 dozens of times, and apparently the Elvis is Alive Museum was there the whole time and I never knew it. So I was glad that Rare Visions gave me the opportunity to discover it. It was there that I scored one of my personal treasures; a T-shirt bearing the photo of Richard Nixon deputizing Elvis as a DEA agent. You've seen the picture. I heard that it is the most requested photograph in the public domain. But the only place I've seen it on a shirt is at Bill Beeny's Elvis museum in Wright City.

I'm wondering, if there's an Elvis is Alive Museum, might there be a Paul is Dead Museum somewhere?

Don CG

The museum features a coffin, a waxy figure and an elaborate theory about what really happened at Graceland back in 1977.

If the exact details of Beeny's Elvis Is Alive Theory don't stick with you, the fried peanut butter and banana sandwiches served in the café certainly will!

Sometimes vehicles in which Elvis once rode are displayed. And Beeny claims that his big, honking sign is the most photographed sign in the world. (Or maybe just Missouri.)

## ROCK OF AGES

Also near St. Louis, but a lot farther from the beaten path than that Elvis Museum, is the Black Madonna Shrine. It's in Eureka, and no, it has nothing to do with that saucy, chart-topping Material Girl. This gorgeous garden of grottos was built to honor Our Lady of Czestochowa, who came to be known as the Black Madonna due to the way she appeared in early paintings.

One Brother Bronislaus Luszcz literally did all the building here, using a sizable hillside on the grounds of St. Francis Monastery as his backdrop. Most impressive of all, he built for decades USING NO POWER TOOLS. It was a lifetime of work, which ended, appropriately enough, one hot summer day in the early 1960's while he was attempting to finish one more piece.

Even if you're not scripturally literate, there's plenty to appreciate about this massive meeting of art and nature. But like the pamphlet says you'll want to "beware of snakes and animals."

## MEET ME IN YOU KNOW WHERE

So far as we know, no one's died yet at the City Museum in downtown St. Louis. But it does have a school bus teetering off the edge of the roof, and quite a few more rough edges than your average theme park. And none of the plastic! The artists who started it wanted to recycle parts of old buildings in creative ways (check out the wall of food trays) and give kids and the terminally immature a place to crawl, slide and squirm around in a variety of small and torturous spaces.

Knowing this, we shouldn't have been surprised that Bob Casselli, the founder of this "computer free zone" couldn't wait to take us to the top of the museum, which is housed in an old shoe factory. Why? To throw water balloons on people below, of course. And we shouldn't have been surprised that he spoke glowingly of someday salvaging old jail cells to give kids a chance to play "lockup."  And building six story climbing walls, and rooftop walkways, and well, you get the idea. Casselli's dreams constitute a virtual vacant lot where imaginations can run wild.

Sometimes we have a hard time saying nice things about our cross-state rival. (They're still testy about losing the World Series.)  But we like the City Museum just fine.          — RM

# St. Louis, Mo. to Beech Grove, In.

*Mike*

## KEEPING AMERICA STRONG

Bill Christman is a two-a-day kind of a guy. Two-corndogs-a-day that is. Christman's on the B & B plan; one corndog for breakfast and another at bedtime, and while that may sound a bit excessive, Ol' Bill knows a thing or two about corndogs that you and I don't.

Bill runs the museum of Mirth, Mystery & Mayhem in St. Louis, located on the 3rd floor of City Museum. Proudly displayed are things like the world's largest pair of underwear, and the honeymoon trailer that Elvis and Priscilla once shared, but it's the siren call of the corndog that floats this boat.

Those lucky enough to pass through the doors are introduced to the "Corndog Path to Total Awareness." It's painted right there on the floor, and even a guy like me with questionable abilities is capable of following along. In short, it's a narrative history of the corndog, with wall reliefs explaining its importance in world history. Ancient tablets removed from a temple in Egypt clearly show a corndog being consumed. A cut away shot of Stonehenge leaves no doubt that early man knew a thing or two about corndog support structures.

A plaque honors the four corndogs of freedom: breakfast, lunch, dinner and snacktime. And there's an early drawing of the Titanic with giant corndog outriggers, a design that apparently cost the boat designer his job at the time. Bill points out dryly that history has since vindicated that man.

But there's a darkside to the corndog as well, and Bill wouldn't be the man he is without pointing this out. Pass through a shadowy curtain, and you're there, in the 6th floor window of the Texas Book Repository. A rifle leans on the wall and spent shell casings lie on the floor. On the windowsill, a half-eaten corndog is testimony enough that the power of the corndog is something one has to respect! Other exhibits about Roswell, New Mexico, Voyager 2 and the corndog conundrum were thrown in for good measure, but to this observer these last ones deserve a penalty flag for "piling on."

Bill Christman says all of his theories intersect, eventually, and at the end of the tour we did some intersecting of our own, as Bill delivered some of those golden goodies right to our table.

I know I'll never be able to look at a corndog again in quite the same way as before.

# IF IT RAINS I'LL BE AT VIRGIL'S

**V**irgil Meyers is like virtually everybody else we meet when we're out doing these shows. He's kind, and gentle, and happy. And his only goal is to brighten your day. If he can't do that with a song, or a joke, or a story of some sort, then he'll take you to the basement and show you his arks.

"I'm 91 years old," he laments on the way down the stairs, "I'm an old man. I

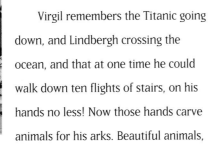

oughtn'ta be a workin'. I'm retired!"

Virgil remembers the Titanic going down, and Lindbergh crossing the ocean, and that at one time he could walk down ten flights of stairs, on his hands no less! Now those hands carve animals for his arks. Beautiful animals, all in pairs. Squirrels and birds and gators and snakes and elephants and giraffes and well, just about any animals you can imagine. And some you can't imagine, because they don't look like any animals I know. Then he paints them and builds them a giant boat, mostly out of scrap wood, so they'll have a home. But at 91, his hands are finally wearing out, he says, and he may not have that many arks left in him.

I left that day with a vision of Noah at the Pearly Gates, a smile on his face, as he reaches out to shake Virgil Meyer's hand some day.

# WHO WOULDN'T WANT TO SLEEP IN A WIGWAM?

At one time, motels in this country were built with a little more character than they are today. Back in the 1930's, long before Super-This-and-Thats and Thumbelina sized "free" cups of coffee, Frank Redford had a vision of Americans traveling the open road, stopping at night to sleep comfortably in his wigwam motels. He built a few of them, but unfortunately for all of us, they never really caught on. We were lucky enough to see one in Cave City, Kentucky.

Now owned by one Ivan John, and listed as a Kentucky historic landmark, this one's been restored just like Frank envisioned it.

"Small, but with all the amenities! And clean bathrooms," Ivan says proudly, and he's not just trying to sell siding.

They are small, but they appear to be very comfortable. Owing to the round shape, the furniture's all been custom-made and it fits nicely in the room. And as promised, the bathrooms were spotless, as well as, well, small. Did I mention that the place had one of those gift shops where considerable chunks of change could easily be left behind? What's not to like?

Be ye child or adult, sleeping in one of these would truly be an adventure, and that's what traveling is supposed to be all about.

## CALL ME A WOOD BUTCHER

ocated just between Hoodoo and Fudgearound, somewhere in western Tennessee, we met a man who claimed to be the original "hoodoo daddy." Now let me just say right here and now that my momma didn't raise no stupid boy, and I know better than to argue with a man who's got a chainsaw in his hand! Hoodoo Daddy it is!

J.L. Nippers is a chainsaw artist. He learned his trade at the feet of Homer Green, a legendary cutter who lives just a short piece up the road in Beech Grove. Nippers makes totems. He makes tables that look like alligators. He makes alligators with wings. He makes snakes, and he makes donkeys, and he makes aliens. Truth is there isn't much he doesn't make. And when he's done, he paints them all up with a nice fresh coat of polka dots -- an obvious incongruity with the lumberjack thing he's got going.

"I just cut out anything people want," he says in all seriousness. "If they want it and I can't cut it out, then it can't be cut out, and that's just all there is to it!"

I believed him. He was still holding the chain saw. And I saw no reason to ask him about the polka dots.  — *MM*

# Marshall, Mo. to Arcola, Il.

*Mike*

## THIS DOG DON'T HUNT

For me, nothing says "America" quite like a town that erects a statue to honor the memory of a dog. We've run across these before; Old Shep in Wyoming, who met the train faithfully every day hoping for his master's return, only to meet his demise under the wheels of said train. Or the statue for Old Drum, in Warrensburg, Missouri, immortalized in a senate speech about man's best friend, a famous case in the annals of jurisprudence.

But there's only one Jim the Wonderdog, and I'll doubt there'll ever be another one quite like him. In Marshall, Missouri, they created an entire park in his memory.

Owned by one Mr. VanArsdale, Jim the Wonderdog was known to dazzle crowds with his uncanny knack for doing all kinds of amazing things. Like picking Kentucky Derby winners, or following commands in foreign tongues, and, according to the signs up in the park, more or less knowing just what you were thinking at any given time. It's said that he could stare a man down, that you couldn't look him in the eye. People from that era like to say "he was pretty near human," but Earl Shannon, who personally knew Jim, saw it differently. "No, I can't agree with that. Some of the things Jim did, a human couldn't do."

Fortunately, he was only used for the good.

JIM
THE WONDER D[OG]

*by*
CLARENCE DEWEY MITCHELL

JIM THE WONDER DOG
1925 — 1937

## SOMETHING TO DO IN THE WINTER

It's amazing what one can do with a Craftsman hatchet. D. Bill, who lives in Bloomington, Illinois, and who apparently doesn't have a first name, is the kind of man who spends his winters in the garage. Working from carefully laid out drawings notated with complicated mathematical equations, the man is a study in patience and tenacity. With pencil and ruler, he carefully transfers the designs he's drawn onto the ends of old wooden street lamp poles, measuring just so, and methodically laying out his lines. Then he picks up his trusty old Craftsman and starts hackin' away.

"If you draw it up, it's got to come out right," he said to us, more than once. Poles line the fences, embedded with Picasso-esque faces that bear witness to this fact. D. Bill says it takes him 3 days to complete a carving, averaging somewhere in the range of 45 to 50 poles each winter, leaving him free during the better weather months to paint them.

He retired in 1982 and succinctly says that he was just looking for something to do, "I can't work outside in the cold, although I've got no heat in the garage. It's something to do in the winter."

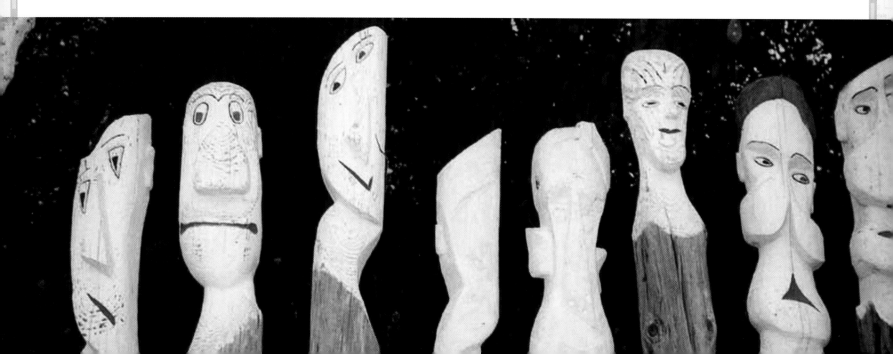

## I LOVE FRESCA

At first glance, Rockome Gardens, in Arcola, Illinois, appears to be a kind of Amish theme park, with buggy rides and gardens, and country crafts. But what caught my eye was the incredible stonework wrapping itself around big plots of beautiful gardens. A man named Martin built these gardens back in the 1940's. Only thing is he made them too big. And that attracted attention. People came from miles and miles around, just to see the gardens with the unusual rock fences, and before he knew it, he had a bona fide attraction on his hands.

The site now covers nearly 15 acres, and you can spend an entire day just marveling at the rockwork. There were flower baskets, birdhouses, archways, even a heart with an arrow through it, which has served as the backdrop of many a tourist photo over the years. The real jewel, however, is a house made of bottles. But this isn't just any old bottle house. No, this house is made of Fresca bottles! Back in 1968, when the local Coca-Cola bottler temporarily discontinued making their lemon-lime nectar of the gods, Mr. Martin became the beneficiary of an awful lot of homeless Fresca bottles.

Some guys have all the luck.

— MM

# Springfield, Il. to Mt. Horeb, Wi.

## COZYING UP TO A CORNDOG

n the road, you eat differently than you otherwise would. One of the things that always look more appealing when you're wheeling around are corndogs. In Springfield, Illinois, Buz Waldmire claims the batter-dipped weenies were invented by his father at the family restaurant, the Cozy Dog Drive-In, that's still proudly making 'em out on Route 66. In the beginning, his dad even carved the weenie sticks himself, and worked tirelessly to perfect his batter.

Cozy Dogs are truly crispy on the outside. And inside there're all the questionable hotdog ingredients that make Don glad he's a vegetarian. As for Buz, he's quite a character. He even talked us into a little manual labor when a new batch of Cozy coating needed to be unloaded.  Just another first for this TV Weasel!

## BIG STUFF

ike and I did wolf down a couple of Cozys (and even Don was tempted), so when faced with another fast food legend an hour or so up the Mother Road, we merely stopped to gawk. The Gemini Giant in Wilmington, Illinois, is a Space Age variation on what insiders call Muffler Men (big fiberglass guys originally built to hold tailpipes.) He's been stiffly standing guard at the Launching Pad Drive-In for a long time now and still looks pretty good. Not good enough, however, to lure us in for a Gemini Burger.

Come to think of it, Illinois abounds with things gigantic—from the World's Largest Catsup Bottle in Collinsville to the Man of Steel himself on the courthouse lawn in Metropolis. And of course, who can resist that bikini-clad giantess who's still selling tires in Peoria?

## AWESOME!

We were headed for Aurora, fictional home of "Wayne's World." It's also the real home to a great display of original outsider art that shouldn't be missed. Its creator, Charles Smith, is a Vietnam vet who admits he had a lot of trouble putting his time "in country" behind him. So he started stacking sculptures in, on, and around his little ranch house. Concrete and scrap metal pieces that examine and explore African-American history and experiences. Some are fun, some troubling, all have a message: Know where you come from. And Charles Smith's yard just keeps expanding, like the jungle that haunts him. Doing this work, he says, helps strengthen the neighborhood, and has kept him from bursting at the seams.

# GETTING THE GRAND VIEW

After our fun but intense time in Charles' yard, we decided some recreation might be in order.  Like some miniature golf...and we knew just the place!  Ahlgrim's Funeral Parlor in nearby Palatine, where as long as there are no services going on upstairs, you're welcome to play a few rounds down in the basement.  Would I make this up?

Then it was on to Wisconsin, where Nick Engelbart found his own "grandview" in the rolling hills outside Hollandale.  After a visit to the nearby Dickeyville Grotto back in the 30s, Nick started building things on and around his own house, often in tribute to the various ethnic groups that settled the area.

Like many grassroots artists, he was a great recycler, with a gentle sense of humor to match his sculptural ambitions.  Eventually, though, the site fell into almost total disrepair, until those preserving knights in shining porcelain at the Kohler Foundation began the restoration process we can all enjoy today.

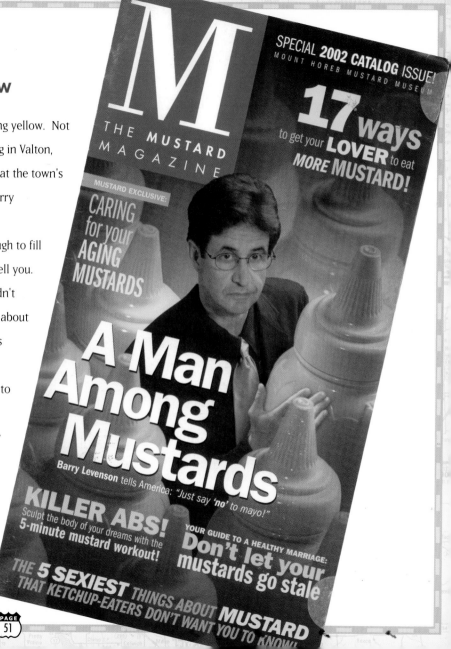

## MELLOW YELLOW

**B**ut by the next day we were definitely seeing yellow. Not at The Painted Forest, an old lodge building in Valton, Wisconsin, notable for its folk art murals, but in Mt. Horeb, at the town's true treasure — the Mustard Museum. Its founder and curator Barry Levenson actually gave up his lawyering career to run the place!

How much mustard can there possibly be, you ask? And is there enough to fill a museum? Well, yes, there are hundreds of kinds of mustard, Barry will tell you.

There's hot mustards, sweet mustards, mustards with names we couldn't pronounce. He's got samples. He's got pictures. He'll even sing you a song about mustard. And if you're lucky enough (we weren't) he might even put on his Mustard Man costume and pose for you.

This man knows mustard and merchandising. So even if you can't get to Mt. Horeb, you can still check out his catalogues.

They're a hoot and a half, whether or not you ever get around to ordering any fiery jalapeno mustard or Filipino chutney. Chances are you'll still end up waving that Poupon U. banner proudly. I know I do. — *RM*

I was indeed glad to cash in on my legitimate excuse not to partake in the All-American cuisine offered at the Cozy Dog Drive In. However, I must say that I relished my time at the Mt. Horeb Mustard Museum.

*Don CG*

# MacGregor, Ia. to Dickeyville, Wi.

## ALL THINGS CONSIDERED,
## HE'D RATHER BE WATCHING GINGER

*Randy*

Surprise is an essential part of our particular approach to show-making. The three of us start with a basic plan and then when unexpected things come along, as they inevitably do, the show often turns out to be better than planned.

Sometimes we're just plain surprised by the terrain itself, as we were in northeastern Iowa. It's nothing at all like the flat cornfields in the other three fourths of the Hawkeye State. There are hills and valleys, even a Pike's Peak named by the same Zebulon Pike we know from

Colorado. And the Mississippi River is far bluer here than the muddy mess it becomes later.

If you're a chainsaw artist in these parts, there's quite a bit of timber to work with. And if you're a chainsaw artist named Dan Slaughter, a self-proclaimed "toothless old bastard," you're content enough with your life as it is not to care whether a vanload of TV guys gets there or not. "I was watching Gilligan's Island. I kinda hoped you wouldn't come," has to be one of the most humbling greetings we've ever heard!

Dan's place is on the edge of a river town called MacGregor, and pulling into his driveway you can see immediately he's not one of those eagle, owl and bear chainsawers. More like Elvis, E.T. and Homer Simpson, American flags, spaceships and dinosaurs. Dan's giant totems are on display next to the garage, -- telephone poles that he's imaginatively nicked, buzzed and shaped into pieces that can't be so quickly explained.

Though Dan is indeed missing a few teeth, you can't help noticing that he's got most all of his fingers. "Is he a folk artist?" That's another of those things he claims not to spend much time thinking about. He'd rather get back to the TV, and hey, "how about a beer?"

## BY THE LIGHT OF THE MOON

The river road on the Wisconsin side of the Mississippi makes for a lovely drive. And it's along that road where Fountain City, Wisconsin, scores points for harboring the tongue-in-cheekiest roadside attraction I've ever seen. The Rock In The House is a pleasant little place that has been smashed to smithereens by a runaway boulder that's still sitting there. You pay on the honor system to walk around and marvel at the luck and marketing savvy of the survivors.

The town of Cochrane is also close to the river on the Badger State side. It's where the Prairie Moon Sculpture Park gives testimony to the creative energies of one Herman Rusch. The Prairie Moon was originally a dance hall that Herman took over to house the things he'd collected, a sort of one-man rural museum. But it's the things he built outdoors to attract attention to his collection that in the end became the real attraction.

For starters there's a long, graceful concrete and crockery fence looping along the road that leads to the Prairie Moon. In the yard, Herman constructed a rambling assortment of towers, spires and even a Hindu temple that looks perfectly at home with farm fields and tall bluffs rising around it. Next to the hall in the shadows of these grand sculptures, there's a simple self-portrait of Rusch, a reminder of how down-to-earth and self-effacing grassroots artists tend to be.

## LOT O' GROTTO

eading further down the river, you can follow the signs on Highway 61 to the Dickeyville Grotto. Dickeyville is the small southwestern Wisconsin town where Father Wernerus and his parishioners built one of the prettiest folk art environments we've seen. Not as big or as majestic as the Grotto of the Redemption in Iowa, the Dickeyville site mixes religion, politics and history in its own fascinating way.

For starters, it's right there on the side of the road, barely set back at all. It sports a beautiful front arch, complete with brightly colored flags made from stones and broken glass. The virtues of patriotism seem to be almost as important here as spirituality, though the overall message is undeniably Catholic. There's even a sign for The Holy Ghost Park!

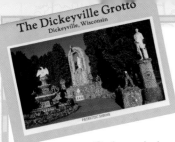

The Dickeyville Grotto
Dickeyville, Wisconsin

Also, unlike Father Dobberstein's exotic rocks and petrified wood, the grotto here seems more dependent on shells and glassware, marbles, and such surprisingly attractive industrial castoffs as gearshift knobs from Model T's.

Maybe because it's so compact and, at least on the day we were there, virtually empty, the Dickeyville Grotto feels more accessible, more human-scaled. Father Gunn, the parish priest at the time of our visit, answered all our dumb questions with patience and good humor, and when we were done cleaning out the gift shop, threw in a couple of ball caps for good measure.

— *RM*

# La Crosse, Wi. to Mitchell, S.D.

Minn.

S.D.

Wis.

Iowa

94

WIS.

29

Minneapolis    St. Paul

SOUTH DAKOTA

MINNESOTA

Cataract

Mitchell

90

La Crosse

Sioux Falls

IOWA

Mason City

NEB.

Sioux City

35

Mississippi River

*Mike*

## BOMBASTIC BOTTLE BONANZA

Paul Hefti is just trying to make the world a happier place, and who can object to such a worthy goal? His backyard is covered with pop bottles. Mostly the 2-liter size. Some he paints, some he leaves clear, and some he letters for making messages.

He says it all started with one little whirligig. When a passerby commented on how nice it was to see such a thing, Hefti was hooked.

For 45 years, he worked at a local box factory, but then he says he got smart, and started working as a full-time bottle artist. Now, it's not exactly clear what it is that prepares a person for a ministry of cheer in pop bottles, but whatever it is, Paul got an extra helping.

His yard is full of life. Pop bottles spin in the wind. They hang from the trees. They perch on his fences, their painted-on faces peering out at the world as it goes by. They line up like soldiers, with messages for passing people; "June is Dairy Month" or "It's Milk" or simply "Good Luck." If you're really lucky, they might even remember your birthday!

The obvious question is: "Who drank all this pop?" One look at Paul,

with his diminutive frame, and you figure it couldn't have been him. But he says he's guilty. And when he's through with each one, he washes it, removes the label, paints it, and finds a new place of honor for it in the yard.

The sweetness revealed in Paul Hefti's yard reminds me that my mom was right. There really is a lot of sugar in pop!

## WALTZING WEGNERS

**N**ext time you find yourself outside of Cataract, Wisconsin, there's a little place on the side of the road you won't want to miss. Paul and Matilda Wegner were immigrant farmers who had something to say, and when they retired from farming, they set out to say it. Lisa Stone, in her book "Sacred Spaces and Other Places" — which by the way is a much more scholarly book than the one you're currently reading — described it as a combination roadside attraction, peace monument, and extremely spiritual place, and she was right on the money.

In 1929, the Wegners visited the Dickeyville Grotto, a hundred miles or so down the road, and it inspired them. Using rocks, concrete and broken glass, they set out to build a place where people could pull their cars over and pass a moment or two in quiet reflection. They built fences and created beautiful gardens. They added picnic tables. They honored the boat that brought them to America — the Brennan — with a replica, and they built a chapel, where all were welcome to worship.

And when they were through, they erected a couple of monuments to serve as their own tombstones, leaving behind a site that left no doubt in anyone's minds that Paul and Matilda Wegner were once here.

## KNEE HIGH BY THE 4TH OF JULY

On my experience, corn grows in fields, or I find it on the table, freshly buttered, thank you. It is not however, typically a building material.

It seems that way back in 1892, aspersions were cast concerning South Dakota's agricultural prowess, and two men set out to correct this egregious error. In Mitchell, South Dakota, they built themselves a palace, and covered it with, you guessed it, *corn*. Lots of corn. And of course, the rest of the story is pretty predictable... So many people came to see the palace that it was obvious to all they'd have to do it again.

So every year, after the birds and the squirrels have had their way with the building, which is in effect the world's largest smorgasbord for critters, the good folks of Mitchell strip off all the corn and start over again.

CORN PALACE

Yellow
Popping Corn

South Dakota Popcorn Co.
Pierre, South Dakota 57501

NET WT. 2 Lbs. (.90 kg.)

Here's the recipe just in case you'd like to try it on your own palace: Start with 275,000 ears of corn, sliced in half, add a ton of nails, and another 3,000 pounds of grain for good measure, then work from June to October putting it all together, and voila, you've got a corn palace second to none! Throw in a gift shop the size of a basketball court, and before you know it, a half million people a year will come to see what you've done. At least, that's how it's worked out for Mitchell, South Dakota.

Sometimes someone gets a crazy notion and a tradition is born.

— MM

South Dakota may seem like a far away foreign land, but it really isn't. If you're from Kansas City, you could have a late brunch, make a beeline for Mitchell, and be eating corn-on-the-cob at The Palace by dinnertime. The place is a thing of beauty and you won't be disappointed. And what a gift shop! As Mike pointed out, it's the size of a basketball court because during basketball season, it is a basketball court. My only quibble with the gift shop where they dribble is that I was unable to purchase a pair of salt and pepper shakers in the shape of ears of corn, which I had earmarked for a friend with a peculiar rare vision of his own.

Don CG

# Baraboo, Wi. to Phillips, Wi.

Phillips

Wis.

WISCONSIN

8

39

Rudolph

Green Bay

94

Wisconsin
River

13

Montello

Lake
Winnebago

Wisconsin Dells

Baraboo

Randy

## QUOTH THE DELLS EVERMORE

What exactly are *dells*? And why does Wisconsin have them? And what do they mean?

Sorry, I don't really have an answer to the first two questions, except that they're a popular tourist destination in the central part of the state, you know... water parks, video arcades and miniature golf.

As for the third question — that's easy. The Dells will always be to me the home of Dr. Evermor (real name Tom Every), an industrial salvager, one-time construction foreman at the legendary House On the Rock, and most impressively, creator of the Forevertron. This sprawling, spectacularly whimsical sculpture may be found at the good doctor's studio behind Delaney's salvage yard outside Baraboo.

The Forevertron is gigantic. It was built from the remnants of observatories and power plants. Solidly built, Dr. Evermor says, so that when the time comes, the king and queen (he's apparently got connections) can launch themselves to heaven from the top of it.

*Juice the gyros and let 'em fly!*

To make that occasion more festive, he's assembled a brass band around the perimeter. And all these crazy musical creatures are in turn being watched by another group of metallic cats and birds!

But that's not all. Dr. Evermor also hopes to make the Guinness Record Book for most sculptures sold. He cranks out hundreds of scrap metal bees, bugs and mosquitoes that he "puts up for adoption" to worthy folks like our own Don the Camera Guy. With his pith helmet, stubby cigar and exhortations to "power on," Dr. Evermor jumped immediately into our RVRR Hall of Fame.

As soon as Dr. Evermor gets enough Juice from Overlord Master Control and all the conditions are right, he no doubt will "Power On" and beam up to the heavens, his massive Forevertron boldly going where no imagination has gone before.

I do hereby reaffirm my pledge to honor and care for my "Lucky Bee", 1996 Species, which I adopted on June 6th, 1997, in a semi-formal ceremony held in a trailer that sits clearly within the cosmic shadow of the 'Tron.

Note that June 6th is the anniversary of D-Day, and now we're all just waiting for our orders. And the good Doctor stresses that there are no rules, no plans, you must "go with the flow" or you lose the energy. And that is quite similar to the way we make Rare Visions.

*Don CG*

## WONDER OF WONDERS

Father Wagner at the Grotto Gardens

When we pulled into the parking lot at the Grotto Gardens in Rudolph, we were greeted by what appeared to be the most undersized marching band in America. Seven or eight sweaty adolescents honking and tooting with considerably more enthusiasm than precision. An auspicious start for our visit to yet another bastion of Wisconsin creativity!

The Gardens were originally the brainchild of Father Phillip Wagner, with lots of help in later years from another priest, Edmund Rybicki. They saw the rockwork and meandering paths they constructed behind the church as a picturesque place for divine contemplation. But it's Fr. Wagner's homemade Wonder Cave that puts this place in a league of its own.

Caves are underground, right? Well, not this one, though it feels like the real thing as you walk inside, winding back and forth for a full fifth of a mile. Along the way bent-over travelers encounter small shrines nestled with statuary and piped-in organ music that sounds a lot like Wrigley Field.

When we finally emerged from an exit at the top of this hand-built hill, we realized it had started to rain. That prompted a hasty retreat from Rudolph that may have caused "someone" to leave Don's prized 35mm camera sitting out in the elements. Believe me, "someone" took a lot of grief for that error in judgment. And still is!

# 'IT'S GOTTA BE IN YOU'

Somewhere past Rudolph, we took another of those unexpected pit stops, spurred by the sighting of Wisconsin's Largest Tree. It would have been just another quick photo op in Montello, but for the appearance of Officer Jack Frost, Wisconsin's Friendliest Cop (and biggest ham.) My ticket-less driving career could have come to an end right there! Luckily, Officer Frost seemed to like us, though I probably pressed my luck asking him to help us load the Big Ball back in the van.

The aforementioned rain forced us to cancel our plans to play catch at Poniatowski, a geographically notable spot where several meridians meet, so on we drove with great expectations, to Phillips. This is one of those places I've wanted to see for years, ever since reading about it in an old Kansas Grassroots Art Association newsletter in the 80's. And thanks to those good folks from the Kohler Corporation, Fred Smith's Wisconsin Concrete Park on the edge of town has been exceedingly well preserved.

Fred Smith ran a tavern, and using its resources, managed to fill a grove out back with statues he built from broken glass and a concrete mixture of his own design. A former lumberjack, he looked back over his life and fashioned a menagerie of animals and townsfolk he'd known, all of whom seem to have a vaguely Eastern European look to them. But the subjects of his artwork also included fishing tales, patriotism and "Ben Hur." Fred loved that movie, and the concrete chariot and driver he built is the highly visible proof!

"It's gotta be in you to do it" is the way Fred explained his passion for creating. And I'm happy it was in him enough to keep breaking those bottles and pouring that concrete. Now if he could just have figured a way to get rid of those buzzard-sized Wisconsin mosquitoes!

— *RM*

# Stevens Point, Wi. to Sheboygan, Wi.

Wis.    MICH.

Marshfield   Stephens Point   Green Bay

WISCONSIN

Manitowoc

Lake Winnebago

Lake Michigan

Sheboygan

Madison   Milwaukee

*Mike*

## THE ANSWER MY FRIEND, IS BLOWING IN THE WIND

I'm a big fan (forgive me) of guys like Tony Flatoff. His yard, which surrounds his modest little house just outside of Stephens Point, Wisconsin, is the kind of a place that always makes me want to stop to look. It's not that it's particularly big or fancy, and it doesn't feature amazing amounts of stonework, or artwork created from broken bottles, or even large metal dinosaurs. It's pretty much just a bunch of fans.

Tony worked at a local hotel for more than 40 years. One day he brought an old electric fan home from work. It was the fan blade he was interested in, because he took it off and hung it on a pole, and the rest is, well, you know.

The fan spun around in the wind and Tony liked the way it looked. If one fan looks nice, he thought, think of how a hundred might look. All you need is a structure to hold them up, and the will to collect all those fan blades. So, with pipes, and poles, and some old wagon wheels, and a keen eye for discarded fans on trash day, Tony set out to create a fan show, for no other reason than to give people something pretty to look at as they drive by. And when they all get to spinning in a good wind, it's truly a sight to see.

As far as I'm concerned, guys like Tony Flatoff make the world a little bit more interesting, and anyone who stops for a look wins!

## ROTTER IS NO NAME FOR A DENTIST

udy Rotter sees art in everything. The 84-year-old dentist, living in Manitowoc, Michigan, is supposed to be retired, but every day he gets up, goes to his studio, and makes art. At last count he had created more than 17,000 pieces, and everyone of them made by the same hands that were once pretty busy yanking teeth in this town.

He used to keep a studio in the basement under his dentistry office, and had a system with his office help. He'd numb the patient, and while waiting for the anesthetic to kick in, go to the basement to work on some creation. When the patient was numb, the nurse would stomp on the floor, and Rudy would come back up. Molars upstairs, stone and wood, and whatever else, downstairs.

"This is my golf, my boat, my fishing, my card playing," he says softly. "I did this while others did those things, and I raised two families along the way. There's nothing more important than family," he said, then leaned over and inspected my teeth, admonishing me to floss more often.

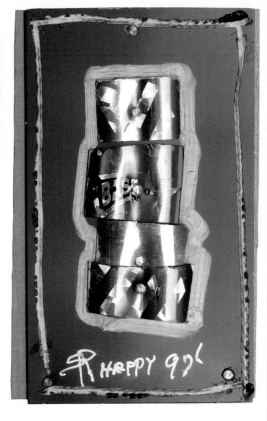

Rudy's feelings about family are evident in much of his work, particularly the carvings. Also evident is his love of the human form. But at 84, the hands that were once so strong have faltered, his joints worn thin from the relentless punishment of a lifetime of carving. But that's only led to a change in materials. He works now mostly with found objects, salvaging this or that and collaging it into new life. And he paints, and he draws and he just generally keeps himself busy. Very busy.

In the process, his museum of art continues to grow. It's on a side street just off the waterfront in Manitowoc. It's not much to look at from the outside, but if you're in the neighborhood, there's a whole other world inside.

Just floss before you go!

## WHEN LAWYERS GO BAD

Clyde Wynia, a retired lawyer, has a whole yard full of critters. He claims he found them, right next door in the marsh. 'Must be why they call it *Marsh*field, Wisconsin, As he tells it, the critters are from the Jurustic period of geo-history, known affectionately to paleontologists as the "heavy metal era."

Clyde is just a little kid in a grown man's body. While we were visiting, he launched a plastic bottle full of water towards the heavens, soaking us all in the process and demonstrating what can only be labeled as a bit of an ornery streak.

He's always had a creative side, and over the years he's expressed it in many ways. He tried ceramics, and stained glass, and they were fine while he was still practicing law. But then, about the time he retired, he took a welding class and discovered that he was actually pretty good at it. He made a large bird and hung it in a tree in front of the house. The grandkids loved it, and Jurustic Park was born.

He filled the place up. Giant dragons with wings spit fire, spade-a-sauruses munch on the lawn, giant creatures hang from trees and there's even a frog band singing away. Often their bodies are really bells, communicating to each other with clangs and peals. And then there are critters science has yet to identify, mounted on springs, flopping this way and that. When they all get to moving in the breeze it's just a little bit disconcerting, but that's the way it is when you're hanging out with Clyde Wynia. You never know when you're going to get bumped by a heavy metal dino, or water bottled, or your leg pulled for that matter.

Another man with too much access to scrap metal, and too much time on his hands?  Not in my book.

## KOHLER IS KING OF THE THRONE

The coolest bathrooms I've ever seen in my life are in Sheboygan, Wisconsin, at the Jan Michael Kohler Art Center. And if the bathrooms are that cool, you can just imagine the rest of the place! These folks know how to live!

Of course, it helps to be a part of the Kohler Fixtures empire, a company with a long tradition of support for the arts, that also knows a thing or two about bathroom fixtures. They built the bathrooms as part of their long standing artist in residence program. And then there's the Kohler Foundation. They've made a mission out of saving folk art sites, mostly in Wisconsin at first, but recently spreading out and beginning conservation work around the country. Many of the sites in this very book are Kohler-sponsored sites, and they definitely do it right.

But it takes more than just a connection. You have to have a vision at the same time, and the Kohler Art Center seems to have plenty of it. From the original Rhinestone Cowboy's house, to the chicken bone towers of Eugene Von Bruenchenhein, to the largest collection of Nik Chand's work ever assembled outside of India, the Kohler folks are true believers, and they've got a collection that's second to none.

We salute them.                    — MM

# Grand Haven, Mi. to Hamtramck, Mi.

*Mike*

## THE HOUSE IS HIS CANVAS

eorge Zysk is yelling at the world. Or at least he was at one time. By the time we crossed his path, in Grand Rapids, Michigan, the carefully thought out messages he'd spent years painting on his house were fading fast.

But you could tell there was a time when George took no prisoners. City fathers, federal officials, presidents and local do-gooders, all were fair game. You could just imagine him up on his ladder, paintbrush in hand, as he took to task the latest target in his sights, for whatever cause he perceived deserving. As a veteran of World War II, George felt like he'd earned the right to be heard, and figured nobody was going to stop him. But zoning boards, city councils, and irate neighbors have all tried.

George has just kept on painting. After all, it is his house and he has something to say.

By the time bad health caught up with him, he'd covered the entire dwelling. Sadly, by the time we caught up with him, the severity of Lake Michigan winters had extracted a dear price, and the house was in decline. Vandals had visited and in a strange piece of irony, had yelled right back at George with spray paint. A new generation at work, I thought. Maybe the community learned more from George Zysk than they thought.

## POLKA DOT IS A PRIMARY COLOR

Heidelberg Street is in the middle of what looks like a war zone, near downtown Detroit, and Tyree Guyton is fighting in the streets. Fighting the drug dealers, and the prostitutes, and the pimps, and fighting now with City Hall too.

Tyree had an epiphany on his front steps one day, and promptly covered his house with found objects. Trash that others had discarded, he re-purposed and collaged as art. And then he did another house, and then another, and at some point he added polka dots, and he announced to the world that this blighted neighborhood was none the less still a neighborhood, and people lived here and called it home. And the city fathers loved him. Art classes made pilgrimages to see the place and newspapers wrote stories about "The Heildelberg Project."

The neighborhood really felt like a neighborhood again, just like the place of Tyree's childhood memory.

But then, just as the riots of 1967 had changed the face of the area, the city's administration changed too. And the new folks wanted to change Heidelberg again. For reasons that remain a mystery, they saw nothing redeeming in Tyree's work. The bulldozers came, taking down whole houses, and buildings deemed

Mike, Jenenne Whitfield, Tyree and Randy at the Heidelberg Project

eyesores. The lawyers came and shook papers, and the surveyors came and claimed land for the city, land Guyton actually had title to in some cases, and more bulldozers came, sometimes in the middle of the night.

But Guyton persevered. He found new things to paint. He hauled 3,000 pairs of tennis shoes home and paved the street with them, just to make a point. He brought home signs and scrap lumber and chairs and old TV sets and just about anything paint will stick to, and he created an

environment that attracted so many people that the drug dealers and the prostitutes were forced to move on. And somewhere along the way, a city administrator made the mistake of referring to Guyton's property as blighted, sending Tyree to the mat.

He'd show them blight. He'd paint polka dots on blight all over the city, and soon buildings that truly were eyesores began sprouting polka dots. Then an amazing thing happened. Other folks picked up their paint brushes and soon paper stands and rotting billboards and abandoned cars and other things not contributing to a better landscape got there share of polka dots, too. Just like in the song folks, "pretty soon it was a movement!"

After all, this was the neighborhood where Tyree Guyton grew up. And he was going to have something to say about that...just all there is to it!

## LOVE & HISTORY — BOTH SERVED HERE

ilvio Barile is up in the mornings before most of his fellow Detroiters. He has bread to bake, and pizzas to make, and people he needs to see. And they seem to need him too.

Silvio likes to sing while he works, with or without customers, and it would be hard to say that he's anything but an artist when it comes to handling the dough. No better pizza has ever crossed these lips. Attesting to this truth is a steady stream of customers that flows in Barile's shop every morning, starting about 10:30. Silvio knows them all. In most cases he already knows what they'll order. He just pulls out his pizza scissors and starts cutting. His customers eye Silvio's pizza the way addicts stare at a fix.

His shop is crowded and small, the walls covered with posters, and homemade signs, little homages to God and country. But step into the courtyard behind the shop, and you step into the past as interpreted by Silvio in mortar.

"It's really no different than making pizzas," he tells me, modestly, "and I like working with my hands."

Barile works concrete like a fine bread dough, and from his hands come the most amazing creations. Sit down at a table out here and you can share your lunch with tributes to ancient Rome, and to the Italy of Silvio's youth, or maybe the Statue of Liberty, or images of justice and equality from the country he calls home now. There's a salute to the Vatican, and to the Holy Grail of hockey, the Stanley Cup, won not so long ago by his beloved Detroit Red Wings. There was even a tribute to Don's favorite knuckleheads, the Three Stooges, and all with an honesty and an obvious passion, a love of great things and people.

There's a song in Silvio Barile's heart as he makes his art and his pizza. And I've had dreams about the pizza. It was that good. Silvio says the secret is the rosemary, but I don't believe him. The secret ingredient is Silvio.

I was born in Detroit and lived there until I was ten. The 1960's were so rough on the city that I used to tell people that my family was from there, but "we got out!" I learned about poverty on trips to Tiger's games at Briggs Stadium — not all that far from Heidelberg Street. This was only my second trip back in 40 years, but I could tell that the social chaos brewing when I left is far from over. In the 24 hours we spent at the project, we witnessed visits by busloads of students from John Glenn High School and bull dozers from City Hall. If the choice were up to me, I'd have to go with the learning experience over the vacant lot.

As for Silvio, he was so inspiring — just a joy. And the pizza was so good that, for the record, I may or may not have let a slice or two of pepperoni slide past my avowed vegetarian lips. *Don CG*

## WELCOME TO THE ART SHOW

ometimes the simplest of ideas can get out of hand. I suspect that Demitri Syzlak didn't set out to create "Disneyland North" in Hamtramck, but then some men are destined for greatness and don't know it.

Decorated with plastic bowls and bicycle rims and fan blades and flying ducks, and a lot of brightly colored paint, Demitri most definitely has the coolest yard on the block. He came here from the Ukraine in 1950, coincidentally the same year that Don was born here, and worked on the line at GM, building transmissions for 30 years. And somewhere along the way, he started building things in his back yard.

A spinning thing here, a whirly-gig there, teeter-totters and helicopters, most of them driven by the wind in some way or another. He liked the Concord airplane so he erected a 12-foot model, painted like everything else, in colors that I like to think of as early fruit salad! When his creations outgrew the backyard he just started building up, over the garage and towards the sky.

But what he seems most proud of is a tattered and torn spiral notebook, full of children's names and notes of joy from those who had visited over the years. That's why Demitri Syzlak never stops smiling. In a country where he'd been welcomed with open arms so many years before, Demitri is just giving back some of his joy.

Lucky me.                                     — MM

# Missoula, Mt. to Regent, N.D.

Randy

## MOOOO! IN MISSOULA

uring our Montana trip, I decided not to shave in order to get in touch with my inner mountain man. Unfortunately, the resulting beard made me look more like a skid row vagrant than Jeremiah Johnson. Oh well, letting the whiskers grow saved ten minutes a day that I used enjoying Big Sky country.

Missoula, Montana, is a college town nestled in the mountains. I'll remember it as the place where, inexplicably, I enjoyed some of the best Cajun food I've ever had. We bought it from a little window at the back of a downtown bar. Who'd of thunk it?

It's also where we met Neil Olsen, a biker who makes sculptures described by one reviewer as "weird and troubling," though he seemed like a pretty nice guy in person. He pointed out that the name "Urethra Park" was somebody else's term for his sculptural endeavors, not something he himself chose. However, the cow in the electric chair and the giant reptile munching a human form by the front fence did display a dark sense of humor.

As for art training, Neil readily admitted that he had none, just an arc welder, a love of model car kits left over from his childhood, and lots of curiosity. Neil did point out that if we planned to stay long in Montana, we might want to do like some of the best known locals have done, and polish up a manifesto or two.

## GOING ONCE, GOING TWICE...

n ot far from Neil's place in Missoula we came upon what was left of Marcus Wolf's Non-Profit Museum. Wolf elected himself "mayor" of his compound, and was a favorite with local artists because of his detailed tours through collections of everything from salt and peppershakers to blow torches. Unfortunately, Marcus passed away shortly before our arrival, and trailers full of his stuff were about to hit the auction block. It was a sad reminder that outsider art environments are often ephemeral, and we're lucky to have experienced and documented as many as we have.

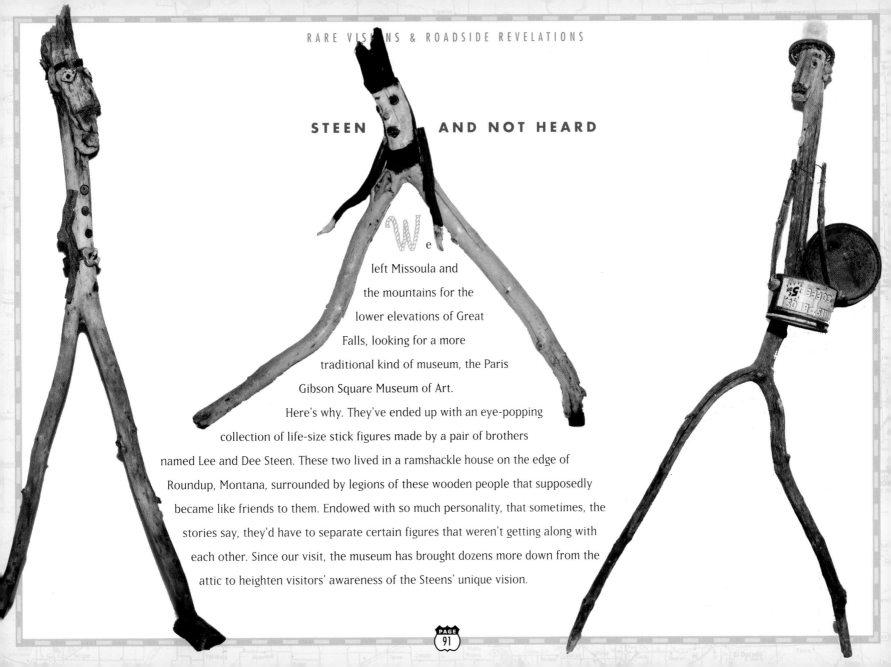

# STEEN AND NOT HEARD

We left Missoula and the mountains for the lower elevations of Great Falls, looking for a more traditional kind of museum, the Paris Gibson Square Museum of Art. Here's why. They've ended up with an eye-popping collection of life-size stick figures made by a pair of brothers named Lee and Dee Steen. These two lived in a ramshackle house on the edge of Roundup, Montana, surrounded by legions of these wooden people that supposedly became like friends to them. Endowed with so much personality, that sometimes, the stories say, they'd have to separate certain figures that weren't getting along with each other. Since our visit, the museum has brought dozens more down from the attic to heighten visitors' awareness of the Steens' unique vision.

## FINDERS KEEPERS

*S*peaking of Roundup, turns out there's more than one reason for going there. Tim Anderson calls it his Little Mansion, and if you like rocks, you're going to like what Tim's done with the place. It features not just rocks — which he's *nailed* to the wall — but wagon wheels, horseshoes, pitchforks, washing machines and other things that people throw away. Tim hauls all these found objects with his bike or tractor, and he uses them to decorate both his home and yard with a designer's measured eye. "I call that the Go-Mobile" he says, pointing out a free form metal assemblage, that he readily admits "don't go." His dream is to build a whole town this way, and perhaps find a wife who might help him accomplish his grand architectural scheme.

# WIMPY WHISKERS AND OTHER WONDERS

tanding next to Tim it became clear how pathetic my beard growing attempt really was. But my compadres weren't feeling much empathy. Not after miles and miles of Montana driving and a night in one of the scariest motels we'd ever paid $29 for. Let's just say that at this point Don was almost finished writing his manifesto!

What else could we do, but drive some more at high rates of speed across Montana rangelands to an all-but-ghost town named Ingomar, looking for a place called The Jersey Lilly?

This 19th century cafè/bar is known round the state for its savory beans. They even sell a special spoon with little stairs on it. You know, so the farts can climb out...

I'll just let you imagine what the next few hours in the van were like.

*Enchanted* isn't necessarily the word I'd use, but it is the name that's been given to a stretch a road we'd heard about in western North Dakota. The Enchanted Highway is of 30-mile length of county road between Dickinson and Regent, so called because of the sculptures that are being erected at regular intervals along it. And they are amazing! A huge grasshopper, a covey of quail that catches the rays of sunset beautifully, a Land of the Giants Farm Family, all erected for no other real purpose except getting people off the interstate. The brains behind this business is Gary Gunther, a former high school principal, who admits some of the local folk think he's crazy. We don't. Like he says, the alternative for little towns like his is to wither and die. "You've gotta do something," is his constant refrain.

And if you do, we at least will come. — *RM*

# Lincoln, Ne. to Alliance, Ne.

## BUMPER CARS

Randy

Lincoln, Nebraska, has pretty well figured out the whole strategy of claiming "world's largest" this or that. For example, the city claims that its O Street is the longest, straightest street in the world. This is a claim that is difficult to dispute, and equally difficult to verify.

Lincoln is also where Loi Vo makes really cool things from car bumpers. Loi came here from Vietnam, and he's extremely proud of a huge American eagle he sculpted that's on display at Lincoln Plating, where he works. For a local high school he fashioned an incredibly graceful knight on horseback. In his front yard, a shiny chrome grasshopper and praying mantis dramatically confront each other. And in each case he can tell you from what kind of car the raw materials came.

He says that big old Mercurys are among the best, but that they're hard to find these days.

While we were wandering around the huge pile of bumpers at his shop, Loi actually let Mike try his hand at some basic welding. We thought for a minute Mike welded his hand and wouldn't be needing that ball glove of his anymore, but it turned out to be a false alarm, and in fact we soon played some wild open-field catch at the Giant Prairie Schooner near Milford on I-80.

## THAT 70s SHOW

After that we buzzed over to Seward, where they say the World's Largest Time Capsule can still be found in the front yard of Davisson's Furniture. It's buried underneath a pyramid, and large enough to hold a Chevy Vega as well as lots of other "everyday items" that got planted back in the 70s. Why? Because they could, of course! We're led to believe that there's actually a bigger time capsule inside a library or something in Virginia, but as far as free-standing-built-for-no-apparent-reason time capsules go, hey, this one wins hands down!

## THINGAMAJIGS AND WHATCHAMACALLITS

*N*ow, you'd expect a town named Mason City to attract *my* attention, but we had another very good reason for going there other than its fine name. We wanted to check out yet another scrap metal sculptor.

Richard Martin's yard is easy to spot in this part of the prairie where foliage starts getting sparse. It's crammed with birds, and bugs, and devils, and skeletons he's fashioned from farm machinery. But unlike some of his scrap-sculpting peers, Dick won't alter a metal part to fit his needs. It has to go onto the sculpture just like it came off the corn detassler or thingamajig, so that someone who'd actually used such a whatchamacallit would be able to recognize it.

Even with all the "junk" ironwork, the Martins' yard was impeccable. And on our way out, Dick suggested we take one of his very cool firebirds with us, further reducing our Chrysler's capacity by another 5 percent!

## ALL-AMERICAN ATTRACTION

We bunked in North Platte, a town that's awash in all things Buffalo Bill. We also spotted a great variation on Lady Liberty here, holding what appeared to be a soft-serve ice cream cone instead of a torch. Our plan was to gas up and head on over to Paxton for an early lunch at Ole's Big Game Lounge. Only one problem: No one had noticed that the time zones change just east of Paxton. Thus we'd gained an hour, which meant there were few signs of life and no buffalo burgers cooking when we hit town about 9:45 a.m.

However, the giraffes, polar bears and rhinoceri on the wall were ready for their close-ups, so Don grudgingly took their pictures along with some good-natured grief from the waitresses. Eventually, we did get some soup, which was quite tasty and fortified us for the long drive through the Sand Hills, past the World's Smallest Courthouse (so they say) in Arthur, and on to Alliance.

Alliance is the home of Carhenge. James Reinders, the guy who built this vehicular version of the mysterious English circle of stones, doesn't live here anymore. But the Friends of Carhenge, like Paul Pheneuff, who showed us around, are darned proud of it. The placement and perspective are identical, but Paul wanted to make sure we knew they "eschew Druids" here, meaning I guess that human sacrifices and such aren't condoned by Nebraskans. Neither are foreign cars. They're all American-made models, all painted the same monochromatic gray.

**CARHENGE**
*&* **Car Art Reserve**

Other auto sculptures have been added to the site, some of them quite colorful. And they've even started featuring musical performances and poetry readings for the public. At the time of our visit I didn't have an original poem of my own to perform, but I have one now: "There was a young Lady from Lincoln..." Just kidding. But not about Carhenge. Roadside attractions really don't get much better than this. — *RM*

As an American, I, too, am in love with automobiles. My father worked for GM and my grandfather worked for Fisher Body. So, this stretch of road and its recurring auto related themes were resonant to me.

Carhenge is perfect. It's out there, it's free, and it's one powerful statement on America's car culture. But I think Randy is wrong when he says human sacrifices aren't condoned in Nebraska. Ever seen a football game in Lincoln?

*Don CG*

# Pueblo, Co. to Fort Collins, Co.

Fort Collins

14

Boulder

Colo.

70

Denver

25

COLORADO

Colorado Springs

50

Pueblo

Mike

## PUEBLO PICASSO

Tony Perniciaro is a painter and a poet. And several lifetimes ago, before moving to Pueblo, he was a bricklayer in New York City. Prolific doesn't even begin to describe the body of work Perniciaro's created, and most of it actually has something to say. Using paint he recovered from dumpsters, he committed his wisdom to paper as fast as he could work the brush. Tony speculates that he's done somewhere in the neighborhood of 100,000 paintings in his lifetime, and at 84, he was still cranking them out.

Tony The Bricklayer
poem-paintings by tony perniciaro

I ran away from home at 47—

the worst catastrophe in history is repetition –

standing forever before a mirror –

He'd published a book once, copies of which he gladly gifted to each of us, mumbling something about it being the 13th sale of the original 10,000 copy run. But later, I discovered that because he was unhappy with the book when it was published, he'd bought the entire inventory, and put them away. It was a children's book, bright with poems and short thoughts, and a peculiar vision of how the world should be. Quite frankly, they seemed like lessons more suited to adults than to children.

But from time to time I still read my copy, anyway.

This stretch of Rare Visions, the show we call "Episode 504", was both the easiest and the hardest one we ever made. And I believe it is the show that I am most proud of.

We discovered Tony Perniciaro, A.K.A. Tony the Bricklayer, and all was right with the world. Tony's art was wonderful, as was his heart. The pictures and sound were all I could hope for and I was reminded of just why I love to do this kind of work.

And then joy turned to sorrow when the camera took a plunge to the pavement. We were six hundred miles from home base with no way to do what we do, and I felt pretty bad. The replacement camera arrived by air with its own set of problems. What was so easy two days earlier became so hard. But Mike and Randy had faith and we persevered all the way to Swetsville. The results became my favorite Rare Visions episode and another strong reminder of why I am, Don the Camera Guy.

Don CG

## THE PRESIDENT SHOOK THESE HANDS

In Denver, we caught up to Bill Potts. He's a big man, with perhaps the biggest hands I've ever seen, but when they wrapped themselves around one of his carvings, they were so nimble and careful they might just as well have been the hands of a surgeon or a concert pianist. With tools that ranged from power sanders to kitchen cleavers, he creates art with old scrap fence posts, and discarded pieces of wood. Carved musicians and presidents, dinosaurs and fish, bar scenes and Zulu warriors, Bill's work was wild and widely varied. There was even a life-sized alligator!

He was invited to the White House once, where he'd presented President Clinton with a sculpture of the prez, playing his sax, and that was something! But two days later, I suspect he was back in his garage, listening to his beloved jazz, and carving away.

Bill Potts isn't a rich man, but he is a happy man. I can still hear his deep down in the belly laugh when I close my eyes. And the alligator will undoubtedly be a visitor in some future dream of mine.

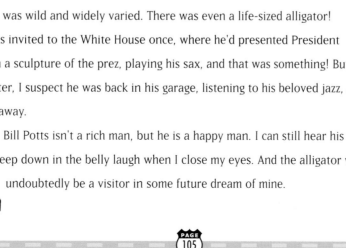

## IT'S A ZOO, MAN

Bill Swets is like a kid in a candy store. He just can't believe how much fun he's having. Just outside of Fort Collins, Colorado, he's opened the Swetsville Zoo. And you get the sense when you talk to him that he's more than just a little bit proud of himself. With good reason. We toured what seemed to be an endless array of sculptures, mostly made from car parts and scraps of steel, and I had the feeling he enjoyed telling us about them almost as much as making them. Dinosaurs were the main course, though bad puns and creatures I couldn't identify were served up with equal joy!

Bill used to be a dairy farmer, and somewhere around 1985, he put a few of his sculptures in the front yard. Lo and behold, people got off the highway to take a look, and he knew he was on to something. When he retired, he threw himself with abandon into creating the sculptures, and before he could say "this is just a hobby," thousands of people were stopping by each year. As he likes to point out "it is just a hobby...it sure ain't a business cause it's got a negative cash flow!"

Now I suppose that one might question the sanity of a man who builds a praying mantis as big as a garage, then plants it next to the house. I, on the other hand, question the curiosity of anyone who could drive by without stopping to take a look.

What would drive an ex-dairyman/volunteer firefighter/seemingly regular kind of a guy to build all these creatures? Bill claims it was simply because he was retired and had too much time on his hands. I think he was bitten by the tinkering bug. And it doesn't hurt that he's got the imagination of a ten-year-old.

What I wouldn't give to have that back sometimes.     — MM

Mike and Randy with Lani Andrews (creator of the "monart butterfly") whose work is displayed at the Swetsville Zoo's Chrome Rose Gallery.

# Sandia Park, N.M. to Beulah, Co.

## TINKERTOWN

*Mike*

A lifetime ago Ross and Carla Ward were circus people. They traveled from town to town, and in between they visited all manner of roadside museums. Then one day they found a lovely spot in the Sandia Mountains of New Mexico, where they decided they would build their very own roadside attraction.

With bottles, concrete, and rocks from the hillside, they crafted a place like no other. Passageways lead up and down, and around, through rooms of miniatures and machines. Calliopes and collectibles, old signs and wagon wheels. Scenes from the Old West, general stores and saloons, blacksmith shops and the Grateful Dead, and, of course, their beloved circus.

The intricate carvings bear witness to Ross's capable hands, and somehow they've managed to tie the whole place together. It's an amazing feat, one Ross sums up with a simple slogan on the wall — "I did all this while you were watching TV!"

Talk about feeling guilty...

## POP SHAFFER WAS ALL OVER THIS TOWN

op Shaffer died long before our van pulled into town, but there's no missing the fact that he once lived in Mountainair, New Mexico. For one thing, there's the Shaffer Hotel, still operating and serving up some mighty fine food. Homemade chandeliers hang from the dining room ceiling, painted with bright colors and symbols reminiscent of Native American traditions. Time may have worn the building a little, but the symphony of color on its ceiling hasn't dimmed one bit. It's not the Sistine Chapel, but that doesn't make it any less lovely. Outside, there's a fence made from concrete and rock, decorated with snakes, horses, owls, and the tree of life, and a sign that announces to the world, "built by Pop Shaffer in 1931."

Just outside of town lies Rancho Bonito, Pop's home and workshop. There's a log cabin, painted with leftover paint from Pop's tractor business. There's a dairy barn with more Native American motifs. There are buildings made of a local rock Pop was fond of using, and decorated with animal motifs he made by slicing rocks in two. And throughout there are comic touches such as little gremlins carrying milk, lending a whimsical quality to most everything you see here.

But here's the amazing part. Pop Shaffer was best known for the "critters" he made out of knurly old beet roots; strange and wonderful creatures that could capture the imagination of both kids and adults. He made hundreds of them. Unfortunately, these were sold off years ago, after Pop's death, by someone with no imagination, scattered here and there, rumor has it, to become a part of some other roadside attraction, somewhere.

## CASTLES IN THE AIR

im Bishop is high, as he likes to say, high on a drug the government can't control. It's called adrenaline and after one look at Bishop Castle in Beulah, you'd get no argument from me. Soaring towards the clouds for some 16 stories in all, it's made from stone; hand selected, hand carried, hand lifted and mortared into place by, you guessed it, hand. Jim Bishop's hands. He's been working the site for nearly 40 years now, that is when he isn't busy fighting with the government about giving it up. It's surrounded by National Forest land, and they've been itching to get his for some time now. But that's another story and it distracts from the sheer magnitude of what he's created.

Sixteen stories tall?  No drawings.  Towers and flying buttresses and rooms of glass and stone?  No engineers. A fire-breathing dragon on the roof?  No plans.

No plans indeed, except for those in Jim's head. And he's happy to lean over and let you inspect his ear, and for just a moment, you have to wonder if you'll see light passing through! He says he's had a better workout than Arnold Schwarzenegger, that each rock has been moved an average of six times, and he knows because he moved them every time! He likes to point out he's not taking anabolic steroids and he just builds what comes natural to him. And he also did all the ornamental iron and spiral stair casings... He learned a thing or two about that at his day job. Did I forget to mention his day job working ornamental iron? I was impressed too.

There's not a square corner anywhere in Bishop Castle, but there's an integrity that people will see long after Jim's gone. — *MM*

Unless they can prove to me that the Pyramids of Egypt were built by one person, I'd have to give the edge in amazing feats of building to Jim Bishop and his castle. Jim did it all solo using only pulleys, ropes, his hands and a pickup truck, starting the year I left the twelfth grade. If only Jim had been looking for an assistant for this project, it could have been my first job out of high school. Talk about your alternate consciousness

*Don CG*

# Catoosa, Ok. to West Mineral, Ks.

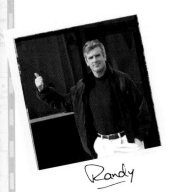

*Randy*

## THAT'S A MIGHTY FANCY WORD FOR YOU KNOW WHAT

Of the many Route 66 landmarks, the Blue Whale outside Catoosa, Oklahoma, is among the most well known. Unfortunately, by the time we saw it, the sun had bleached it to a somewhat, uh, lighter shade of whale. Still, the remains of the old Blue Whale swimming hole speak of a gentler time. And our visit there actually allowed me to use the word "ambergris" in conversation. (It means *whale puke*. You can look it up.)

A lighter shade of whale? Why, I oughta... Perhaps Randy should take the backseat for a while. Maybe yes, Moby no.

This stretch of the show felt the most like three guys out for a good time. Could be the Route 66 factor. To me, nothing says "we ain't bound for WallyWorld" better than that old highway.

*Don CG*

BLUE WHALE

Collinsville is just a few miles from Catoosa, and is home to a prime example of what scientists might call *toolfencis maximus*. In other words a really huge fence made from things that were just lying around. Like tools. Apparently, a blacksmith named Madison started it, and later a guy named Jack Metcalf liked it so well he decided to keep expanding it. Eventually it was got about as long as a football field.

Some parts of the fence are easily recognizable — pumps, wrenches, tire irons and so forth. Others require an intimate knowledge of farm machinery and oil drilling rigs that I hope and expect I'll never have.

Jack was as gracious a host as you could ask for, answering our city boy questions patiently and giving us a short cut to our next stop — a place I knew was going to be a real jaw-dropper.

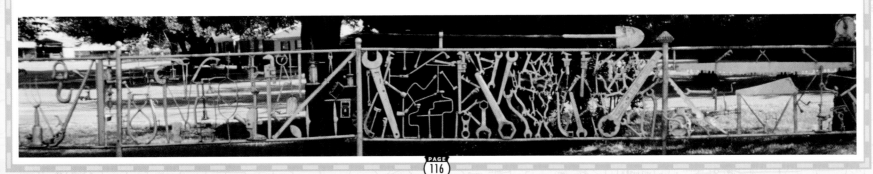

# FIDDLIN' AROUND

I wasn't let down.

Ed Galloway's Totem Pole Park is three miles outside Foyil on Highway 28A. In the 1920s and '30s, Ed taught industrial arts at a nearby state school. But in his off-hours, using a lot of concrete and even more ingenuity, he built a genuine roadside attraction.

At the time Route 66 ran right by his place, and the six-story cement totem pole he fashioned as the centerpiece of his park must have been hard to miss.

Sprinkled around the big one were other smaller, equally colorful totems, a picnic area and his aptly named Round Room built to display violins Galloway also made (of wood, not concrete.)

Totem poles and violins are an unlikely combination. And even though Ed isn't a Native American, his appreciation and artistic use of Indian symbols and imagery hit home. His totems may not be authentic Native American art but they are uniquely American in their own way.

Jim Reed, Randy, and Carolyn Comfort, of the Rogers Co. Historical Society

# A WHOLE NEW MEANING TO THE PHRASE 'CHAT ROOM'

eading north from Foyil meant hooking up with the Oklahoma Turnpike, whose toll system confuses me to this day. "If you just read the signs, it all makes sense," the surly attendant told me." Not true. We did break loose from it near Miami, then followed Old 66 again past the eerie-looking "chat piles" of Picher, an unintentional monument to bad mining practices. Practices so bad that the debris left behind has left the town surrounded by a lunar landscape.

It gave us something to chat about as we drove back into southeast Kansas, where another highway landmark stands next to the road in Riverton. Eisler Brothers Grocery claims to be the oldest continuously operating business on Route 66. This place is a throwback to the general store days of yore, and its Scott Nelson loves to talk and sing. "Route 66" of course! After a few spirited choruses, the conversation turned to another local legend — the Four Corners Spook Light that's fascinated folks down here for years.

Is it swamp gas, reflected headlights, angry spirits or UFO's? Well, all I can tell you is that we gamely followed our guide out into the darkest pitch-black middle of nowhere, saw absolutely nothing, and lived to tell about it.

A lifetime of hard work and the liberation of that retirement brings the flow of creative juices. A few years back we met a man named Robert Dorris who has filled his farm yard in Erie, Kansas, with giant reptiles and dinosaurs composed of car parts skillfully welded together, much to the cost-free delight of both small and rather large children.

"I've probably worked harder since I've retired," Robert told us, "That's usually the case. Like they say, if you've got anything you need to do, you'd better do it before you retire because you won't have time afterward."

And that's pretty good advice. And who knows, maybe I will. I've got plenty of time. That just might be the most important lesson that I have learned from Rare Visons.

Don CG

## WHITE CASTLE, NO ONIONS

At our next stop, Pittsburg, Kansas, we learned an important lesson. When a motel advertises a "construction special" the rate can't be nearly *special* enough. After saws and hammers and non-working air conditioners woke us far too early, we set out to see what I call "the Flying Nun House." Locals call it The Castle.

It was built by a lawyer back in the '30s, using recycled materials, and its odd shaped roof and unusual angles definitely make it a one-of-a-kind residence. Plus its owner at the time also happened to be an expert on Hance White, an early 20th century stoneworker/folk artist whose carvings and marblework still adorn buildings and tombstones around town.

## NOW THAT'S *BIG!*

But it's outside Pittsburg a little ways, in West Mineral, that we found an attraction that dwarfs just about all other roadside wonders. An attraction that transforms grown men into 10-year olds again. An attraction called Big Brutus.

It's a giant electric shovel (that's right, electric) that towers above its surroundings in the field where its owners unceremoniously left it after years of service back in the '70s. And the good folks of West Mineral have turned it into a showpiece. The World's Largest Tonka Toy! You can actually sit in the shovel's cabin and pretend you're scooping or smashing anything or anybody you want. This baby could do it, and no one could stop you.

For a 10-year-old grown man that's about as satisfying as it gets.

— *RM*

BIG BRUTUS
*Explore it!*

Biggest Attraction in Southeastern Kansas

6 Miles West of K7 & K102 Jct.
then 1/4 mile South
West Mineral, Kansas

Phone      316-827-6177

Fax        316-827-6174

Dedicated To
The Mining Heritage Of
Southeast Kansas

# Springfield, Mo. to Eureka Springs, Ak.

Mo.

Springfield

Ark.

44

Republic

60

Highlandville

MISSOURI

65

Mark Twain Nat'l Forest

Mark Twain Nat'l Forest

Branson

62

Eureka Springs

ARKANSAS

Rogers

Mike

## PAINTING A SONG

Robert E. Smith is a man after my own heart, because we have something fundamental in common. We both like to sing. At least, I like to think I'm singing. Randy and Don may beg to differ. And though he may not be any more blessed than I am when it comes to the ol' pipes, Smith certainly has bigger dreams than I. Someday he hopes to sing the national anthem at Busch Stadium in St. Louis, before a big league ball game. For now he's singing in Springfield, Missouri.

Turns out Robert E. Smith can paint too. Seems he's been painting

since childhood, except that in those days, he likes to point out, he was painting with crayons. The water and oil paints didn't come along till later in life.

He paints his friends, and he paints things he sees on bus trips, and things he sees on TV or in books. Colorful and sincere, his work has a child's innocence, a playful quality that soothes the soul. And he paints on nearly any surface; cardboard, canvas, even an old missile. He'd painted one when we were there, an homage to Khrushchev, Castro, and Kennedy, "The Big Three," as he put it.

One minute I'm a mere passenger, semi-content in my ignorance regarding our next stop, hurtling down the highway only half-wondering what Messrs. Mason and Murphy are planning. Then, before I know it, I'm face-to-face with a character like Robert E. Smith and I am suddenly and most definitely engaged.

Robert is a ball of energy, and even a nasty nick from a shaving accident is not about to inhibit him as he imparts his story to us in song and paint. As a favor to him, I tried not to photograph the Band-Aid on his lip, but he simply moved too fast for me to focus my camera on one side of his face as opposed to another. I don't expect it mattered much to him anyway.

*Don CG*

After completing each painting, he makes an audio tape explaining who the characters in the painting are and what they're up to, for the benefit of whoever is lucky enough to end up with the painting.

And of course, every tape comes with a song or two, crooned by Robert E. Smith himself. Talk about "value added!"

## OUR LADY OF THE PHONE BOOTH

t's not just signs that boast "world's biggest" that compel us to exit the highway. "World's smallest" will also do the trick.

In Highlandville, Missouri, Bishop Karl Pruter has built the world's smallest church, and that's the story he's sticking to. It seats 15, though I'm not sure that "comfortably" is a word I'd use in this case. I will say that I've never seen a smaller church. Preuter saw a picture of a blue cupola once, in a magazine, and he says he said right then and there, "Hey, if I put one of those on my old washhouse, it'll look just like a church."

One blue cupola, some beautiful gardens, and a custom-built teeny tiny pipe organ later and Karl was Bishop of the world's smallest church. Bishop Karl says, "we're just trying to serve people." And I like to think they're doing it in a really small way!

## SCULPTURES GROW IN THIS GARDEN

alph Lanning used to build casings for cement work. In fact, he helped make the power plant smokestack you can see from his backyard in Republic, Missouri.

He bought the land back in 1963, and in 1970, just before he retired, or "got tired" as he likes to say, he began sculpting.

"I just started in, that's all," he says, giggling, "I just put em together and they wind up that way — just junk, all it is."

He laughs a lot. And it's quickly apparent that the one person most entertained by the Ralph Lanning Sculpture Park is Ralph Lanning. Sculptural highlights include Paul Bunyan's wedding ring, Lady Godiva on horseback, a series exploring the concept of the first broken heart, and creatures made out of farm implements and old scrap metal. If you set them in motion, they're kind of springy, which would also be an apt description of Ralph himself.

There's a miniature town in the backyard, and a two-headed dinosaur out front near the road. And there's a confusing story attached to the dinosaur about water running in two directions from the very point where the dinosaurs stand, baffling to a mere mortal like me, but Ralph tells the story with such joy that it doesn't really seem to matter if it's understood or not.

His wife Gretchen, who makes mighty fine throw rugs, says, "Ralph never sits still for two minutes. If he's in the house 'cause it's storming or something, he just paces back and forth."

People driving by stop on a regular basis, just to take pictures. And Ralph Lanning has a smile, and a story, for everyone who stops.

# ROCK SOLID

Elise Fiovanti arrived in the Ozarks during the Depression, and settled just outside of Eureka Springs, Arkansas, where she married one Albert Quigley and raised a family.

Now Eureka Springs is an interesting story in and of itself, with several claims to fame. Known as the "Little Switzerland" of the Ozark Hills, it's a town where no two streets intersect at right angles. It's also home to a church that you enter through the bell tower, and it has a seven-story hotel where every floor has a ground floor exit. But my favorite town attraction is Mrs. Quigley's Castle.

In 1943, Mrs. Quigley asked Mr. Quigley to build her a new house. Because she loved nature, she designed the house with 32 glass window boxes. But alas, the Second World War intruded, and glass was being strictly rationed. Mr. Quigley saw no way to get the needed materials, and the building of the new house was postponed.

One day Mr. Quigley left for work, and upon his return discovered that Mrs. Quigley had up and moved the entire family into the chicken coop, and she and the kids had torn down the old house. That's how Mrs. Quigley got her new house, and that might have been the end of this story, except she didn't stop there.

Seems that one of the things the Mrs. liked most about nature was rocks, and she'd been amassing her own collection since an early age, so rocks became the primary building material and artistic motif on the Quigley estate.

"This was her utopia," granddaughter Debbie Quigley told us, "her dream come true. And her true obsession was collecting. She never carried a purse, instead she carried a bucket for collecting rocks!"

She added rock walls, and rock goldfish ponds, rock planters and rock birdhouses. She crowned the rock walls with beautiful old bottles, and she even made rock poles and attached bottles, her version of the oft seen bottle tree.

She liked to "rock" things she appreciated. One day she stepped out of a favorite pair of old shoes in the garden, and she rocked them in. Apparently, everything was fair game for her rockin' ways.

Mrs. Quigley may have set out to build a house, but there's no doubt that she ended up with a castle!

— MM

# Beaver Lake, Ar. to Stuttgart, Ar.

Randy

## LORD, MAKE ME AN INSTRUMENT

No, not Hogs Crawl, Hog Scald. They used to herd the hogs into this ravine, and scald the hair off before they butchered them. So it came to be known as "Hogscald Hollow." Ed Stilley is trying to explain the strange name for this lovely piece of Ozarks land tucked into the edge of Beaver Lake. It's where Ed has lived more than half his life, and where, for the last 20 years or so, he's been making some very unusual guitars. At least I've never seen guitars with saw blades, gears and kettle lids in them before.

Ed's been a preacher as well as a farmer, and this guitar-making thing began, he says, when the Lord offered to help him through some hard times if he'd try to build an instrument. Ed, who'd had no experience at such things, plunged in, made the first one, and has been at it ever since. By now, there've been hundreds, he figures, all given away to kids in the area. "Money won't buy 'em" is how he puts it.

And on every guitar Ed inscribes the same Bible verse. Want one without the verse? Sorry, Elder Stilley says, "they sell ones like that at the store." When he has the time, Ed hauls them over to serenade the residents of a nearby nursing home. It may not be the sweetest sound they've ever heard, but it's heartfelt, and like Ed says, "I never play the same song twice."

## IN A PIG'S EYE

Speaking of unusual place names, this area's rich with them. Hogeye, for example, is just on the other side of Fayetteville, a few miles from what's left of Bug Scuffle. Back to the east, outside Conway, sits perhaps our favorite: Toad Suck Park. Vast tracts have been written about how that name was derived. Everything from French mistranslations to drunken ferryboat captains. Frankly, I don't care how the name came to be. It's just fun to say.

Conway is also where we met another of those prolific sculptors who didn't start out as one. Finton Shaw has the upper body of a stevedore or ironworker, which just happens to be the occupation he's had most all his life. But after some heart attacks in his 40s Finton started thinking more about the big picture, and using his skills to make art exploring life's larger questions. The pieces are right there in front of his welding shop at the edge of the highway, and continue on into a sculpture garden he's built in back.

This is where things really get interesting. Take "Cosmic Love" and "The Girl From Madagascar," for example. They are, well, by Arkansas standards fairly explicit explorations of sexual themes and the human form. "I'm probably the only ironworker around here who reads a lot of mythology," Finton tells us, while admitting that he tries not to overthink the pieces either. "I just do what trips my trigger." Like a lot of the untrained artists we encounter, Finton enjoys getting a response from people who inevitably pull in to take a look. "One guy asked me if I was playin' with a full deck, or on drugs? I told him 'neither'."

Finton Shaw was standing amidst the materials of his trade; the stacked I-beams and weighty pile of heavy metal as he pondered his artistic future.

"I don't want to be moving this stuff around when I'm sixty," he said. I couldn't resist telling Finton that I was considering getting into welding so I wouldn't have to be hauling this heavy television gear around when I'm sixty.

And who knows, by then maybe I'll have an assistant, and I'll be Don the Cinematographer Guy.

Don CG

# SEEING AIN'T BELIEVING

orth Little Rock resident Audrey Burtrum-Stanley calls that other place across the river "South North Little Rock." Audrey's never at a loss for words. And she was happy to use a few showing off such sights as The World's Second Largest Sundial, which she helped get built. She's also seen to it that a famous local tree didn't get razed to make way for a road, by cleverly giving it legal jurisdiction over itself.

Best of all, she's also the resident expert on the Old Mill, a North Little Rock landmark that has to be seen to be believed. But Audrey says don't believe it, because "it's all fake." That is, it was built to look like an 1832 mill in 1932, by a Mexican artist named Donicio Rodriguez. Rodriguez also employed his "el rustico naturale" technique in Memphis at Memorial Cemetery, but I like his work at the mill better.

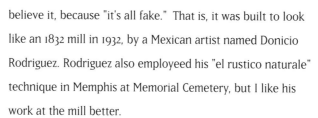

Not just the very elaborate mill, but the fallen logs and faux branches all made with concrete, and particularly an arched bridge that looks like something from an Edgar Rice Burroughs illustration. Apparently, Rodriguez was a secretive guy, who worked without a mold, and kept his materials in the trunk of his car, leaving behind this jaw-dropping reminder of his skills.

Oh, if you're a "Gone With the Wind" buff, you might appreciate this trivia tidbit about this "unreal" place. It appeared in the opening credits of the movie for 8 1/2 seconds, even though it's nowhere near Atlanta.

# FOWL BALL

Before leaving, we crossed over into "South North Little Rock" to play catch in MacArthur Park with Russell T. Johnson. Not the Russell Johnson who played The Professor on "Gilligan's Island", but the one who's put together a heck of a website about his home state. It's got photos and essays and all sorts of information about Arkansas oddities, all of which we used liberally in making our show. Russell's a little leery of media folks, and after zinging a few heaters at us in the park, I suspect he might have been nursing an aching arm as well. Check his site out at http://www.aristotle.net/russjohn/index.html

It was Russell, in fact, who tipped us off to the Coat of Many Duck Heads in Stuttgart. Roughly an hour from Little Rock, Stuttgart is rice-growing country, and maybe not coincidentally, a great place for duck hunting! Seems that a duck dresser there named Ruby Abel (also a champion duck caller) decided to make a coat (size 10, we think) from the very colorful mallard heads that were normally being tossed aside. She wore it in her café, and around town, and now it's the centerpiece at the Stuttgart Agricultural Museum. Or at least we thought so, though the nice ladies minding the store that day pointed out that most people really come to see the Waterfowl Wing and the hundreds of duck calls they've got on display.

But then, we're not most people.

— RM

Frances Camp with Mike
and the Coat of Many Duck Heads

# Huntsville, Tx. to Houston, Tx.

Randy

## EVELYN AND HER LAWN BOYS

We left Huntsville, home of the Texas State Penitentiary, in search of the Texas Sacred Gardens near New Waverly. And we found them. We also found the small but powerful force of nature named Evelyn Blazek, who's kept the Sacred Gardens going. Evelyn and her late husband John started building the shrine decades before as an expression of faith that their son, who was critically ill at the time, would recover. He did.

The Blazeks built their grottos and displays with old bathtubs and washing machines, indoor/outdoor carpet and cast-off lampposts, pieces of culvert pipe and whatever else Evelyn could talk someone into giving

OUR LADY OF GUADALUPE

her. "I'm very persuasive," she told us. Which she proved by convincing Mike and I to mow her lawn!

Evelyn hated to see us, and our free labor, depart. But Houston was still an hour or more away, and storm clouds were gathering.

Houston is a mecca for folk art fans, in large part because of the Orange Show, which, though it is located just a few miles south of downtown, might as well be in another universe.

## MY FAVORITE FRUIT

The Orange Show in Houston is very simply, the late Jeff McKissack's tribute to his favorite fruit. That doesn't mean, however, that it's all orange. It's mostly white in fact, with lots of colorful designs and detail work, much of it made with items that McKissack proudly salvaged from other Houston landmarks. He built it several stories high, not unlike a fortress, to help create an image of oranges as strong and powerful, capable of making all of our lives better, if we'd just let them. Jeff thought this message would be so well received that the Orange Show would rival the Astrodome as a tourist attraction.

It didn't quite work out that way.

THE ORANGE SHOW

The Orange Show Foundation, which maintains the site and keeps Jeff's dream alive, has since established the annual Houston Art Car Parade as an event of major proportions. Every April hundreds of wildly decorated vehicles barely resembling the machines they started out as, descend on the city for a weekend of revelry. We missed it by a couple of weeks, but Ripper the Friendly Shark (who began as a Toyota Corolla) did drop by for a visit. The Big Ball of Tape even hopped in his jaws for a joyride, but discovered the truth in that old adage... The ride was great. It was the stopping that hurt!

## BLOOMING GENIUS

The city of Houston has no zoning laws, which may account for some of the unusual things that regularly pop up here. For example, the two elaborately constructed houses that Cleveland Turner a.k.a. The Flower Man has created. Called the Flower Man because of his way with blooms, Turner rides around town on his bike to find materials that he can put to colorful use. He must have been out on the prowl when we came by because we didn't see him. But we did talk to a neighbor across the street who agreed that the houses were really something to look at. And a lot better for Turner, according to the neighbor, than "the drinking" he used to do.

## 99 BOTTLES OF BEER ON THE WALL, AND THEN SOME

Which brings us to another of Houston's attractions. One that owes its very existence to drink. Specifically, beer. John Milkovisch, the site's creator, not only consumed beer, he decorated with it. Eventually, the entire house he shared with his wife Mary was — most attractively, I might add — covered with beer cans. Milkovisch sliced and diced them, made shingles and shutters and window casings, and even passed the idea down to his sons, who continued to adorn the trees and fences around the house after he died.

"He didn't drink it all himself. I helped," Mary said to us with a wink. And of course once the word got out, people brought "supplies" for John to work with. It's like an encyclopedia of brewing right there on the walls, from cans of Billy Beer to exotic imports you've never seen before. And how about this?  Owning the World's Only Beer Can House also gave Mary a really great reason to refuse anytime someone tried to sell her siding!  — RM

*Mary & John Milkovisch*

# DeKalb, Tx. - Beaumont, Tx.

*Mike*

## MONGO GRATEFUL

eKalb, Texas, is the boyhood home and final resting place of America's favorite plus-size TV cowpoke, Dan Blocker. You just knew that all was right with the world when Ol' Hoss tossed another bad guy into the horse trough each week on Bonanza. In real life, Dan wasn't afraid to take a stand either. He was so disgusted with Richard Nixon at one point that he left the country, which makes him a winner in our book! And I have a theory; Alex Karras owes his acting career to Dan Blocker's early and untimely death.

We left a cup of coffee and a cookie on Hoss's grave, just in case Hop Sing's not doing the cooking in heaven.

BLOCKER

B. DAN D. BLOCKER
DEC. 10, 1928
MAY 13, 1972

## STAGG PARTY

At the end of a long and winding lane sits the house that Charlie Stagg built. It's a sprawling complex of beams and bottles and concrete, with a big domed building that serves as his studio, built on land that once belonged to his mother, some 13 acres of trees, surrounded now by the boom that is Beaumont, Texas. Charlie built it himself, hauling all the materials in by hand, and, as he likes to say, beating the snot out of himself in the process.

"I just built it. I didn't relate to anything, no measurements or anything. I built it under the influence of watching little bitty old bugs; you know the way wasps make their nests. They taught me how to be able to work along and get something done. You just stay at it. You don't stop and you get something done," he says with a seriously contagious laugh for punctuation.

Charlie's not only a house builder, he's an artist as well. He creates DNA-like strands from whittled wood, then paints them with bright colors. They twist and turn, and take on a very organic kind of nature, and in a sense the house is just an extension of that organic nature.

Charlie told us that his place, tucked back in the swampy woods, was a magnet for neighborhood kids with healthy senses of adventure and vague senses of property rights. And not all of them were showing the utmost respect that Charlie's endeavor deserved. They would find walls made out of bottles just too tempting a target. Conventional resistance was futile. So Charlie would instead invite them into his unique world, and sure enough, they would become friends.

*Don CG*

Charlie slept and worked out here for 15 years. Of course, he was younger then, and as he likes to point out, a person can sleep anywhere, even in a log, with the aid of enough beer. And an artist must have materials to work with! But open heart surgery has a way of changing one's perspective, and habits, and though he's given up the beer for now, one look around and it's easy to see that the soldiers didn't die in vain. Walls made of bottles run in all directions, with small rooms for sleeping and meditation lying at the ends, making it hard to tell if there's a front or a back, or even a side for that matter. Charlie says he's pondered that very notion, from time to time, and it doesn't really matter. The house just is. Like something found in nature, something wild.

It's no ordinary place, that's for sure. But then, Charlie Stagg is no ordinary man.

## I'LL HAVE FRIES WITH MY HISTORY

Sometimes you find the most interesting things in the most obscure places, and Beaumont, Texas is one such place. It's home to the J and J Steakhouse, which features the "Eyes of the World," an homage to great places around the world. It was created by one John Gavrelos, a Greek immigrant who never forgot where he came from, nor the things in life that were truly important to him.

As the story goes, John once worked in a candy factory, somewhere in Louisiana, where he apparently took a shine to the candy molds. He wondered why they couldn't be made out of wood, and before you could say "Hershey," he was whittling away. Using old cigar boxes, plywood and crates, he set out to leave a record of the wonderful things he'd seen in his life. The Parthenon, the Acropolis, the Statue of Liberty, and grand cathedrals, among other things. All carved with incredible accuracy, and mostly from memory. It's just a steakhouse on the side of the highway, but there's history there, and one man's lifetime of memories recorded in wood.

## IT'S NO CHRYSLER

Xmeah ShaEla'ReEl is just looking for a little attention. Not for himself, mind you, but for the good word of the Lord. With oil paint and glitter he paints fire and brimstone, and claims he's put more than a million highway miles on this very van.

"I like to call it the burning bush effect. From a distance, it's just this big old bright ball of color, and it draws you in. You can't help but look at it. And hopefully you'll slow down a little while you read it, maybe be a little safer out there, when you're driving."

But Randy is always a safe driver, and that's a really good thing, since he hogs all the driving!  Motion sickness my ...        — MM

# Chauvin, La. - New Orleans, La.

*Mike*

## ANGELS HERE ON EARTH

It's hard to believe that one man could turn out as much work as Kenny Hill has, but then a lot of his story will seem like fiction.

Kenny Hill is a bricklayer by trade. One day, for who knows what reason, he started working on a sculpture. It was a self-portrait, and he told a neighbor that if he liked it when it was done, he was going to make more. He must have liked it, because for the next 12 years, between bouts of earning a living, he toiled away on a small plot of land, just off a bayou, in Chauvin, Louisiana.

Working in concrete, he built life-size figures, telling his version of the story of salvation. There are angels holding horns, and angels with sand clocks, angels with swords, and angels playing harps, and then more angels after that. There's Christ on the cross, and the Gates of Heaven. There are lost souls, world-weary people, and there are self-portraits of Kenny, along the path at various stages. And, as you might expect, there are the Gates of Hell, as a reminder of the wrong path.

In the back of the lot, in a little detour from the theme of spiritual redemption, there's a lighthouse that stands 50-some feet tall covered with an extended relief of American history; cowboys and Indians, the flag raising at Iwo Jima, jazz bands and bald eagles and girls in bikinis.

The one problem with all this is that Kenny Hill didn't own the land his sculptures were built on. And after a dispute with the landlord, reportedly over the mowing of grass, Kenny Hill walked away from his beloved art. He just up and walked away, after 12 years of work, and he's never been back.

Now that might have been the end of this story, as it often is with such places. Someone comes in with a bulldozer, and just like that it's an empty lot, waiting to be sold. And that's in fact what nearly happened here, save for one good man, and a good foundation.

The one good man is Dennis Siporski. He teaches art at Nicholls State College. It's just up the road apiece, and he'd been to visit the site on various occasions over the years. He'd even spent time with Kenny himself. A neighbor called Dennis and warned him of the impending doom, and he set out to do the right thing. As luck would have it, Dennis had worked for the Kohler Company back in college. He remembered their interest in this kind of work and brought it to their attention.

The Kohler Foundation subsequently stepped in and bought the place, and it wasn't long before they had conservators on site, and crews shoring up the bayou dykes, and a plan and the funds for turning Kenny Hill's masterpiece into public art. And in a strange piece of irony, they didn't want to own it either. As is their custom, the Kohler folks deeded the property to an interested community group. In this case, Nicholls State University, who'll administer the day-to-day concerns.

Dennis Siporski says that Kenny Hill wouldn't even have considered making a sculpture for money, though he'd gladly lay bricks for you. He said it would ruin his spirit. He created his art for the community and for the sheer joy of it, and for whatever other personal reasons he may have had. And it wasn't for sale.

I have to believe that Kenny would have approved of what Kohler has done. After all, they just want to be sure his work is around for people to enjoy for a long time to come. And they were willing to back that up with their wallet.

HOUSE OF SHARDS

## NO PLACE QUITE LIKE IT

f you have three of something, it's a collection, and if you have four or more, it's a *foremost* collection, at least according to John Preble, and he ought to know; he's the curator and owner of the UCM Museum, in Abita Springs, Louisiana. John likes to say that if he were a millionaire, he'd only hire someone to do the books, because he'd still want to be the curator here, and it's easy to see why.

This place has a little bit of everything, and a whole lot of some particular things, including what just might be the world's largest collection of paint-by-numbers art. John points out that it was only after spies from the Smithsonian saw his collection that they put on a show of their own, the bitterness evident in his tone. He takes solace in the fact that he never paid more than a dollar for any of his, and that his museum is a little different than the Smithsonian.

"No tax money was wasted here," he's quick to point out

And then there's the Bassigator, captured, he claimed, from the swamps near by. Half bass and half gator, it's a homely old thing, sure to give the kiddies a pleasant night's sleep. And I have to mention the quackigator, because John's real proud of that too. Half duck and half gator, it took third prize at the county fair in taxidermy, which would have been more impressive if it hadn't been the only entry. And what's not to like about the only museum on earth with proof that the Eisenhowers were actually aliens.

There's a house out back covered completely in glass shards, and a camper with a UFO on the roof, and there are plenty of other things to while away a minute or two, but the featured attraction at the UCM may just be a room full of miniatures, a tip of his hat to Ross Ward's Tinkertown in New Mexico. John carved these with his very own hands, which are healing nicely, he adds.

John Preble likes to think of himself as a marketing genius, at least that's what he says. But then, we had to point out that a "marketing genius" might have come up with a better name than the UCM Museum. He claims it was actually suggested by his son, but he quickly points out that the boy's doing better now, in his new digs at the county home.

"I like to torture him when I stop in on visiting day. Someday son, this will all be yours!"

Run, don't walk, to the UCM museum, if you're ever in the vicinity. They've got really cold pop and the bull**** is included in the $3 admission. Can you believe he still calls to remind us we forgot to pay?

## THE LAND OF NEW ORLEANS

As anyone who's ever been there knows, New Orleans is a whole other country. We could have spent weeks there shooting shows, but for us staying anywhere for more than a day can be dangerously close to overstaying our welcome. So we just made two stops in the land of nasty coffee and deep-fried dough balls with fancy sounding names.

Dr. Bob, who we theorize was never given a last name, was kind enough to have us out to his warehouse studio, just on the edge of the quaint but oh so smelly French Quarter. Over the years, he's made a habit of wandering the quarter, picking up things other folks throw away. Old signs, or ironing boards, or miniature toy pianos; it's all fair game for becoming Dr. Bob art, and his studio is thick with the stuff. He likes to paint as well, and he's got a slogan that's become legendary in folk art circles, "Be Nice or Leave." You can't hardly turn a corner, or trip over a wino, without seeing the slogan in some shop, all framed up nice and neat with pop bottle caps round the edge.

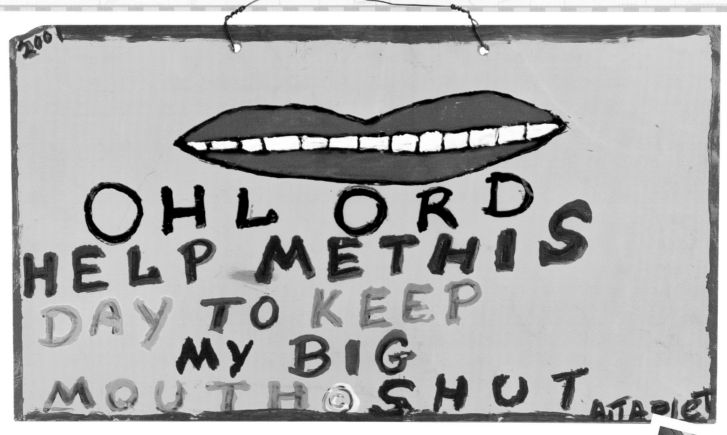

200

OHL ORDS
HELP METHIS
DAY TO KEEP
MY BIG
MOUTH © SHUT AITADIET

Al Taplet, on the other hand, is a guy who shines shoes. Big Al, as they call him, though he really wasn't all that big, dispenses wisdom on slate roof tiles and just about anything else that will stand still long enough to be painted, when he's not polishing leather. He had a slogan as well, "Oh Lord help me this day to keep my big mouth shut," and you couldn't miss it no matter which way you turned. He claims his work is neo-primitive African American street art, but to me it seemed mostly like plain old good sound advice. Unfortunately, none of us were wearing dress shoes, though I know I've got a pair somewhere, but that didn't stop Big Al. Being the creative kind of guy that he is, he was more than happy to lay an oiling on our ball gloves.

It was a sacred kind of moment in the city of the all night party, a party that we were apparently not invited to! — *MM*

# Ocean Springs, Ms. to Vicksburg, Ms.

Randy

## GOOD GIG

was standing knee deep in the warm Gulf Coast waters of Ocean Springs, watching a sailboat glide by in the distance, when I realized why people think I've got a pretty good job.

Of course, for most of the day we'd been racing around on hot Southern highways in search of a really big chair that would, at best, end up getting 10 seconds of TV time. And just outside Gulfport we found it! We looked at it. And we left.

We also found the Walter Anderson Museum, which was a big deal for Mike, who'd been profoundly affected by a documentary he saw during his formative weasel years. Anderson was a painter who threw

himself into his art. For years he would row a small boat 10 miles out to Horn Island, where he could literally immerse himself in the natural world that he painted. He also made elaborate murals, sculptures, and ceramic works, all on display here. While Anderson was scholastically trained, the museum curator readily agreed with Mike that the man really was a "visionary," and a good choice for our show.

# IT'S NOT THE HUMIDITY, IT'S THE HEAT!

As tropical as the Mississippi coast feels, once you drive inland, the terrain begins to look almost Midwestern. It seemed like that around McComb, Mississippi, which we recognized as the home of the Rhinestone Cowboy, Jimmy Bowlin. Or at least it had been, until his passing. Now his entire house, along with his rhinestone-encrusted car, clothes and teeth have been moved for posterity to the Kohler Art Center in Wisconsin.

We'd come to McComb because a woman named Bette Mott has a self-professed "flair for decorating." She's crammed every room in her house to the ceiling with dolls and doilies and gingerbready bric a brac. But because Bette had been hospitalized earlier in the week, we had to take our tour of the house with Betty guiding us over a cell phone!

This cutting-edge technological ploy worked fine, except that whenever we plugged in one of our lights, the circuit breakers popped. Oh, and the camera shut down in response to the Southern heat. Pretty soon we were several hours behind schedule, which really became a factor down the road when some ominous storm clouds began gathering above us outside Natchez.

## EARL AND JOE

We wondered if we'd make it to Earl Simmon's place in Bovina before the heavens let loose. And again, we lucked out. The very moment we pulled up, the deluge began. But Earl is the kind of guy who doesn't freak out over a few drops coming in, even though his art, painted on scraps of wood and roofing tin, is displayed there.

You see, Earl expects a leak or two. He built his rambling three-story treehouse totally from scratch, a room at a time, from leftover lumber and metal that he's turned into viewing rooms and narrow winding stairways — even a little dance floor. But tonight the DJ booth isn't working, and given the way water and electricity have been known to get along, maybe that's just as well.

Earl and his artwork (he particularly likes to paint food) have gotten a lot of support over the years from the Attic Gallery in nearby Vicksburg, which deals in so-called "outsider" artists. Being Sunday, the gallery was closed, but the coffee shop downstairs did serve up the best cup o' joe I'd had in weeks, and one of the patrons provided us with directions for the quickest way to reach Margaret's Grocery out on old Highway 61.

## 'PRECIOUS IN HIS SIGHT'

ood thing we didn't need actual groceries. Because you can't get them at Margaret's Grocery anymore. Margaret's out of that business. But with her second husband, the Reverend H.D. Dennis, the store has become a unique, brightly colored means of spreading the Gospel, as the signs say "to Jews and Gentiles."

The Reverend's in his late 80's and can't hear very well. However, he can still outpreach just about anybody. During WWII he was trained as a bricklayer, and he says the pinks, yellows and reds he's painted this place with should remind people that "you can't have a bouquet of flowers without different colors. We're all God's children."

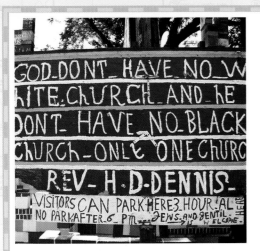

GOD DONT HAVE NO WHITE CHURCH AND hE DONT HAVE NO BLACK CHURCH ONLy ONE CHURC REV H D DENNIS VISITORS CAN PARK HERE 3 HOUR AL NO PARK AFTER 6 PM JEWS AND JENTIL WELCOME

IT IS WRITTEN MY HOUSE IS THE HOUSE OF PRAYER

THE TEN COMMA DMENTS OF GOD

ALL IS WELCOME GOD HATESIN REV. H.D. DENNIS

Along with the distinctive towers that flank the complex, and the scriptures that adorn the walls, Reverend Dennis has outfitted an old school bus with an altar, and decorated it like no other. Imagine an explosion at the Pez factory. Unfortunately, the wasps like it too, and with the temperature inside pushing 110, staying "on the bus" much longer would have had us all speaking in tongues!

— RM

# Oxford, Ms. to Cullman, Al.

Randy

## NUTS TO ME

If you're having problems with your Chrysler mini-van, I recommend you take it to Chandler Motors in Oxford, Mississippi.

Since Memphis, we'd been hearing death-rattle sounds coming from the right front wheel, and they kept getting worse! By the time we reached Oxford, where William Faulkner has a smelly little alley named in his honor, we could no longer ignore the thunk-a-thunks.

We'd had car trouble before. Once, surveying all the goofy stuff attached to the front bumper, a mechanic in Kansas had told us, "Ya'll may wanna move that dog. It's blockin' the air."

We found this to be good advice. But this time we feared we were going to need to do something more drastic.

Well, Galen and the other guys at Chandler Motors are an honest bunch. They pointed out as how we could spend a whole lot of money letting them poke around underneath for a few hours, or we could just tighten the lug nuts and get back on the road.

Anyway, there we were, flying down the highway, lug nuts freshly tightened. When we noticed that another car had raced up behind us flashing its lights and honking. Turns out some idiot (that would be me) had left our cell phone on top of the van. This friendly Mississippi motorist happened to notice the phone flying off the van roof as we picked up speed, whereupon he retrieved it and chased us down.

Talk about your Southern hospitality.

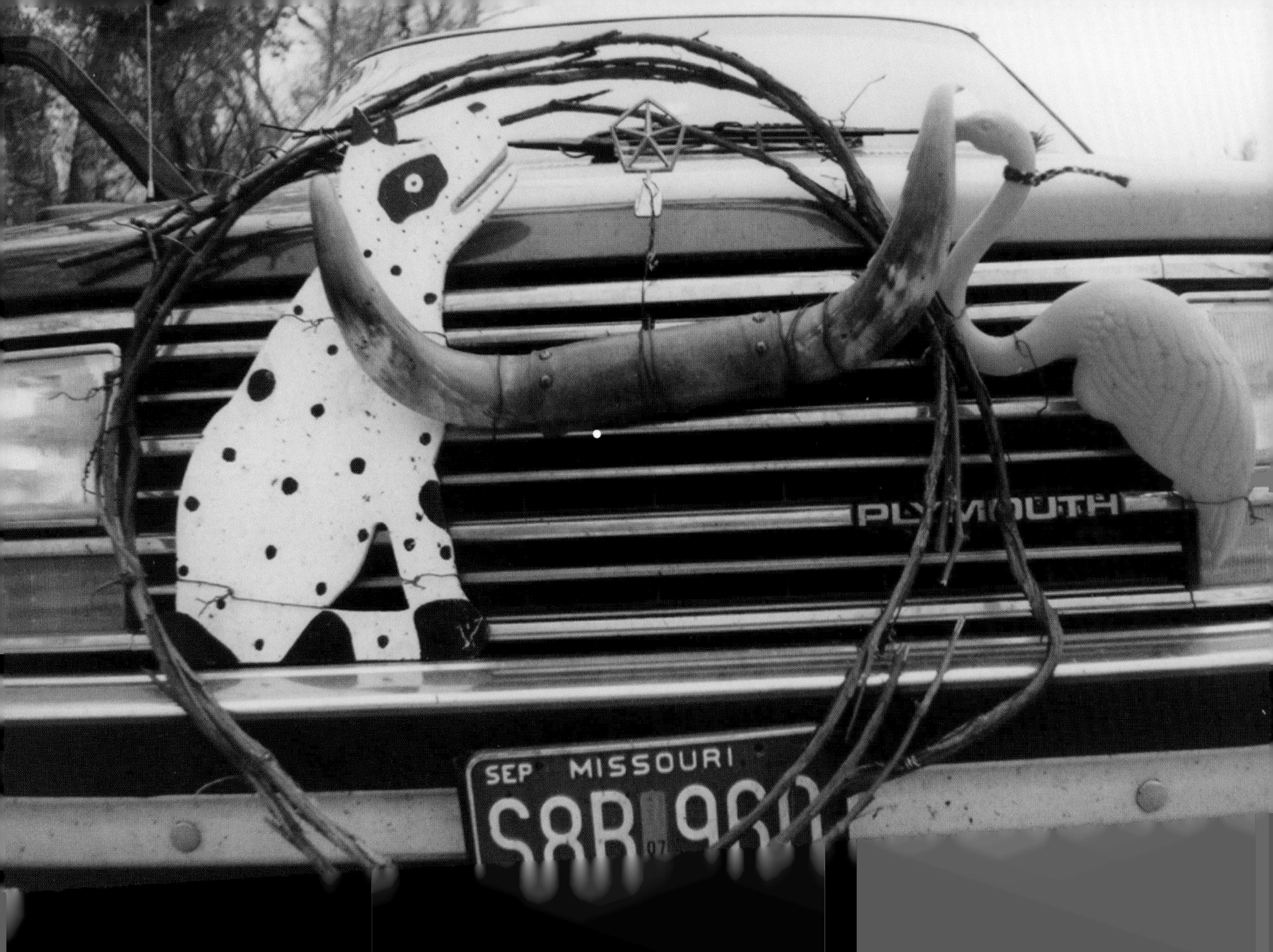
PLYMOUTH
SEP MISSOURI

## SOLE SINGER

There were no other incidents on the way to Kosciusko, though there was more kudzu, that insidious southern vine, growing along those roads than I thought was possible. Then in Kosciusko, at Mrs. L.V. Hull's house, we encountered more shoes, signs, and other odd stuff crammed into one small space than I thought was possible. We're talking wall-to-wall artwork, arranged with barely enough room to squeeze through between the piles.

L.V. is often referred to as "the shoe lady" because of her way with footwear. But shoes, it turns out, are just the tip of the iceberg.

She figures that all kinds of things other people don't want are just the things she needs. The slogans on her many hand-painted signs express her attitude nicely and concisely. For example, "Friends Are Hard to Find, Mind Your Business!"

We sat with L.V. on her front porch as she spoke of some pretty rough times she'd seen in her life. Then she teared up as she sang a little gospel tune. Making her art, she told us, has helped her laugh and has brought people to her house from all over the world. People, like us, whom she'd never have met any other way.

## POUR A LITTLE SUGAR ON IT

immie Lee Sudduth has one of the best laughs I've ever heard. It sounds like a string of firecrackers popping inside a tin can. And Jimmie laughs a lot.

We found Jimmie, who's well into his 80s, working in his little studio in Fayette, Alabama, just past another of those Jitney Jungle convenience stores that proliferate down here. Dirt, sugar and house paint. Those are the key ingredients in the stark, earthy paintings that have made him one of the best-known, best-selling "outsider" artists around.

"Gotta be that good Alabama dirt" he explained, as he slopped the paint mixture around in a big white bucket on the floor. In addition to being a painter, Jimmie is known as something of a musician, though his doctor told him to put away his harmonica for health reasons. That didn't keep him from dancing some wild steps for us in the front yard. He also wanted to be sure we saw his scrapbook, proving how many pretty girls had stopped to visit him over the years. Apparently, this artist gig has its perks.

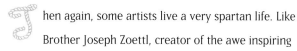

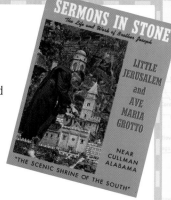

# WHOLLY HOLY

hen again, some artists live a very spartan life. Like Brother Joseph Zoettl, creator of the awe inspiring Ave Maria Grotto in Cullman, Alabama.

Brother Joseph came to America in the early 1900s with serious health problems that left him small and misshapen. His condition, however, did not prevent him from working long and arduous shifts at the power plant at St. Bernard Abbey. Nor did it deter him from creating a spectacular grotto replete with miniature versions of hundreds of the world's great sites and cities.

He built them into the side of a sizable hill on the monastery's grounds. Except for a few nearby landmarks he'd actually seen, his miniatures were all based on postcard images or pictures in books. There's the Holy Land, scenes from Egypt, Verona, Italy, and even the Alamo. Sometimes the scale is a little off, or some detail missing because, it seems, it wasn't in the picture he used as a reference.

The Ave Maria Grotto is one of those places where the whole is truly greater than the sum of its parts. We've seen more intricate pieces, and more grand ones. But the effect of walking through this place, imagining all the work and dedication that went into its creation, leaves one speechless.

In the gift shop they show a vintage newsreel that helps put it all in perspective. In flickering old footage, you see Brother Joseph, kneeling as he attends to one of his miniatures. He stands up and smiles, serenely surveying his tiny hillside world. No words are needed.        — RM

Perhaps the second most asked question I'm asked, right after "What's with that voice?" is, "Why so many grottos?" And the answer is simple. "No two are alike." The Ave Maria Grotto just kept unfolding before us. Monroe, our guide at this stop, said you can go through here twenty times and still see something you missed the last time. The sad thing is that I only had an hour or two to try and capture the place on videotape. I have to believe that I'll get another stroll down those paths someday.        Don CG

# Pittsview, Al. to Summerville, Ga.

Mike

## THERE'S ONE BORN EVERY MINUTE

Sometimes this job is just plain too much fun, and guys like Butch Anthony are the reason why.

There must be something in the water in Pittsview, Alabama, because folk artists abound in those parts. Butch is one of 'em. He pulled up in an old hearse, his Alabama Mamma Jamma mobile, which was decked out with critters on the roof, and words of wisdom and wit painted on the windows. He told us he once drove it all the way to California and back, some 6,000 miles, and even got married in it along the way.

"I went through one of those drive-through windows out in Vegas," he says, totally deadpan. "Went in for a Big Mac and come out with a whopper."

Butch was wearing an oversized pair of overalls when we met him, with a few well-placed holes for ventilation. Of course, there was a story that went with those, too, but good taste prevents me from sharing the details of that story just now.

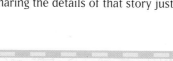

Butch likes to wander the swamps of Alabama, looking for roots of trees that remind him of people. With a little paint and a bit of imagination, it's surprising just how much like Jane Fonda a tree root can look. James Brown, too, for that matter, complete with a bird's nest hairdo. And just about anything else he picks up along the way is raw material, from old toilet parts to discarded suitcases, they're all just art, waiting to happen.

Butch hails from Seale, Alabama, where he owns and runs the Museum of Wonder, a collection of buildings filled with exhibits of the weird and wonderful, and a sign out front ordering "high fluten art dealers to stay away."

"It used to be a quarter to get in," he says, "but now it's just a dollar." (I'd parted with my dollar by the time I figured that one out.)

Butch's museum would make P.T. Barnum green with envy. Among the exhibits were Elvis's pelvis, nose hair from the Loch Ness monster, the world's largest gallstones (removed, not passed), and the one and only Mile o' Mo Bird, found only in the swamps of Alabama. It flies straight up then dives down beak first, burying itself halfway in the swamp mud, after which it proceeds to whistle Dixie from the wrong end. According to Butch, again with that straight face, you can hear that bird for darn near a mile o' mo.

What a joker.

## THIS GARDEN GROWS CROSSES

Mister W.C. Rice is a Jesus man. On a corner lot, out where the suburbs of Prattville, Alabama, have recently encroached, W.C. has laid out a message for all to see. He calls it The Miracle Cross Garden. Through sheer numbers, a certain forthrightness, and an unusual use of old appliances, he's managed to create another one of those sites that can't be missed.

And that's just what his new neighbors are unhappy about. They'd like it gone, and have even attempted to buy him out. After all, they're building some pretty nifty places in these parts now. But W.C. has an answer for them. There's a sign up that says, "For sale-5 million dollars-Cash," and just past that one there's another one.

"New price-for sale-25 million dollars," and that's W.C. Rice's final offer on that matter!

## ST. EOM LIVES

**E**ddie Owens Martin built one of my favorite sites, and led what was perhaps one of the stranger lives we've come across on our journeys. In the 1930's, as the story goes, after years of living on the streets of New York, he came down with a severe case of pneumonia. Bed ridden for a long time, he claims he died, and a giant appeared before him, giving him his vision for The Land of Pasaquan.

And then came the rebirth.

At the age of 49, he returned to Buena Vista, Georgia, where he'd grown up and where his parents still lived, christened himself St. EOM from the initials of his name, and with a sixth grade education, and knowing nothing about line or form, proceeded to turn four acres or so into an incredible labyrinth of walls, reliefs, buildings and gardens.

Mixing concrete, he used hubcaps, Tupperware, trash can lids, pots, pans and almost anything else he could find as molds, and he built his vision, telling fortunes on the side to pay the freight. It was a magical place, painted in bright bold colors, like something you'd expect to find in some palace from the Far East. Posts with the faces of giants watch over the entrances, and geometric shapes repeat down the walls, creating vivid patterns of adornment. Snakes lie on top of the walls, serving as railings in a sense, and symbols of good luck according to legend. And Eddie apparently had a way with snakes, because the locals say he used to put radios at the base of the trees, calling the black rat snakes down with the vibrations from the music. There were cosmic mirrors, and meditation chambers, and even a dance pit before he was finished, all contributing to what I can only say is one of the most mystical places we ever visited, the Land of Pasaquan.

Eddie never called any of it art work. He preferred instead to say it was "just a lifetime of hard work." And of that there can be no doubt.

APRIL-1-1993
PRESIDENT ROSEVELT

BY. HOWARD FINSTER FROM GOD MAN OF VISIONS.
GOD CREATED ALL ANIMALS FOR ALL PEOPLE- SOME FOR
WORK ANIMALS-SOME TO GIVE MILK- SOME TO GROW
WOOL- SOME FOR HOUSE PETS- AND WATCH DOGS- SOME
FOR TABLE FOOD- AND ON- MAN KIND DID NOT COME
FROM MONKEYS- OR ANIMALS- MAN IS HUMAN NOT
ANIMAL- MAN WAS CREATED BY GOD- IN GODS- EMAGE
FOR GODS. GLORY, MAN IS OVER ALL ANIMALS NOT UNDER
THEM. HUMAN BLOOD- AND ANIMAL BLOOD DONT. AGREE
DONT. MIX- GOD MADE 4- BLOODS- FISH- BLOOD. FOWL- BLOOD
ANIMAL BLOOD- HUMAN BLOOD. IF THEY DID MIX- THERE
WOULD BE NO ORIGINAL CREATURS ON EARTH- Howard

Howard Finster TO DON

## PREACHER MAN RULES!

Howard Finster was the Chairman of the Board when it came to visionary art. He spent a lifetime down in Summerville, Georgia, turning what was once a swamp into an art site of the highest order. Along the way, he created album covers for groups like Talking Heads, and books were written about his work. And all the while he was preaching the Good Word.

Finster's concept was to make a garden where every kind of edible fruit on Earth would be grown. A showplace if you will, which took on a radically different character than was originally imagined. Eventually it took a different name, too: Paradise Gardens, reflecting a lifetime of visions that Howard said he always had. In his own quiet way, Howard Finster took what the rest of the world discarded and made it the cornerstone of his message.

"I was raised up fooling with junk," he said quietly. "I always liked to see what I could do with junk, what I could make out of it."

Along the way he took to painting as well. Angels and Bible verses. Personal messages from Howard himself about life. All emblazoned on pieces of plywood or Masonite or whatever else he had lying around. And he made these available to his visitors so people could take home a small part of his world.

Howard held court in front of his Paradise Gardens, in the later years mostly just on Sundays. He'd play a little guitar, he'd sing, and he'd preach a little scripture. And we were blessed to have seen it all.   — MM

Howard Finster is about as close as we have come to encountering a real celebrity on our travels. The lifetime project that he calls a "museum of the invention of mankind" covers the spectrum of Rare Visions from junk to religion. As our good luck often goes, Howard arrived with a banjo and a prayer. A segment on our show usually lasts about four or five minutes. I must have shot five or six half-hour tapes because I was lucky enough to be able to.

Howard told us how he was working in his garden one day when he sensed the presence of the late Elvis Presley standing behind him. "I didn't know what to say or what to do because I'd never had the dead standing behind me like that before. And I said, 'How about staying awhile with me?' And Elvis said 'Howard, I'm on a tight schedule.'"

Well, so were we, but I think The King may have made a big mistake.

# Addresses

These listings are accurate to the best of our knowledge. Things change, so best of luck...

## ALABAMA

### Alabama Museum of Wonder (pg 172)
41 Poorhouse Road
Seale, AL
334.855.9547

### Ave Maria Grotto (pgs 168-169)
St. Bernard Abbey
1600 St. Bernard Dr. S.E.
Cullman, AL
256.734.4110

### The Miracle Cross Garden (pg 173)
1330 Indian Hill Road
Prattville, AL
Northwest of town on Hwy 82 and
left on Co. Rd 86. On private
property. Please view from the
street.

## ARKANSAS

### Coat of Many Duck Heads (pg 135)
In the Stuttgart Agricultural Museum
921 E 4th St
Stuttgart, AR
870.673.7001

### Finton Shaw (pgs 132-133)
5080 Hwy 64 West
Conway, AR
501.329.0709
www.fintonsculpture.com

### Giant Popeye (bonus)
Alma, AR
Across from the
high school, in
front of the
Chamber of
Commerce.

### MacArthur Park (pg 135)
East 9th Street
Downtown Little Rock, AR
Also contains a memorial to the
state's first human dissection.

### The Old Mill (pg 135)
Lakeshore & Fairway Ave
North Little Rock, AR
In the Lakewood Residential Area;
off of State Hwy 107.

### Quigley's Castle (pg 128-129)
274 Quigley Castle Rd
Eureka Springs, AR
4 miles south on Hwy 23
479.253.8311
April 1 - October 31
Closed Sundays and Thursdays
www.quigleyscastle.com

### Ozark Shoe Tree (bonus)
Hwy 187, 1 mi from Rt. 62
Beaver, AR
Strange tradition of throwing
footwear up into folliage.

### World's 2nd Largest Sundial (pg 134)
North Little Rock, AK
At the foot of the Broadway Bridge.

## COLORADO

### Bill Potts (pg 105)
Denver, CO
Potts can be reached through the
Colorado Council on the Arts
303.894.2617

### Bishop Castle (pg 112-113)
Route 615
Beulah, CO
On the edge of the San Isabel Forest
970.484.9509
http://bishopscastle.freeservers.com

### Genoa Wonder Tower (bonus)
I-70 exit 371 (Hwy 109)
Genoa, CO
719.763.2709
See seven states and room after
room of amazing collections.

### Swetsville Zoo & Chrome Rose Gallery (pgs 106-107)
4801 East Harmony Road
Fort Collins, CO
970.484.9509

## GEORGIA

### Paradise Gardens &
### Finster Folk Art Gallery (pgs 176-177)
84 Knox St
Summerville, GA
Garden: 706.857.2926
Gallery: 706.857.2288
www.finster.com

### Pasaquan (pg 174-175)
Buena Vista, GA
From the Town Square, drive north on Georgia Highway 137. Less than a mile away, Highway 137 forks to the left. Take the left and then take the second paved road to the right, C. R. 78. In half a mile, Pasaquan will appear brightly on the right.
912.649.9444

## IOWA

### Albert the Bull (pg 25)
East Division & Stadium Drive
Audobon, IA

### Dan Slaughter (pgs 52-53)
3279 Kline Brewerie Road
MacGregor, IA
319.873.3711

### Grotto of the Redemption
### (pgs 22-24)
300 N Broadway Ave
West Bend, IA 50597
515.887.2371

### Memorial Fountain (bonus)
John Brown Park
5th Street
Humbolt, IA
By Fr. Dobberstein, creator of the nearby Grotto of the Redemption.

### War Memorial (bonus)
Old Rolfe, IA
3 miles north of Rolfe, IA.
By Fr. Dobberstein, creator of the nearby Grotto of the Redemption. (Good luck finding it)

## ILLINOIS

### Ahlgrim's & Sons Funeral Home
### (pg 50)
201 N Northwest Hwy
Palatine, IL
847.358.7411

### Charles Smith (pg 48)
126 S. Kindoll
Aurora, IL
Private residence, please view from the street

### Cozy Dog Drive-Inn (pgs 46, 51)
2935 S 6th St
Springfield, IL
217.525.1992

### Gemini Giant (pg 47)
Launching Pad Drive-In
810 E Baltimore St
Wilmington, IL
815.476.6535

### Max Nordeen's Wheel Museum
### (bonus)
Woodhull, IL
So many items you'll be "maxed out."
309.334.2589

### Rockome Gardens (pg 45)
125 N County Road 425e
4 miles west of Arcola, IL
217.268.4216
Open mid-April thru October Special Christmas Show in Nov. & Dec.
www.rockome.com

### Superman (pg 47)
Town Square
Metropolis, IL

### Uniroyal Gal (pg 47)
1800 SW Washington Street,
Peoria, IL

### World's Only Hippie
### Memorial (bonus)
Arcola, IL
Bob Moomaw's tribute to the Spirit of the Sixties.
www.hippiememorial.com

## KANSAS

### Atomic Cannon #1, (bonus)
Near Fort Riley, KS
In "Freedom Park," at exit 301 of I-70. Built in the mid-50s to hurl nuclear shells far enough that they wouldn't kill the people who fired them, probably.

### Big Brutus (pg 121)
West Mineral, KS
Six miles west of the junction of K 7 and K 102, then 1/2 mile south
620.827.6177

## Boyer Gallery (pg 10)
1205 M. Street
Belleville, KS
785.527.5884
Closed: December — mid-March
www.nckcn.com/boyergallery

## The Castle (Flying Nun House) (pg 120)
601 Grandview Heights Terrace
Pittsburg, KS
Currently uninhabited — however, may be viewed from the road.

## Chase Co. Courthouse (bonus)
Cottonwood Falls, KS
Built in 1871 in French-Renaissance-style.

## Davis Memorial (pg 6)
Mt. Hope Cemetery
606 Iowa St
Hiawatha, KS
785.742.7643

## Dinosaur Not-So-National Park (pg 119)
North of Hwy 47
1 mile west of Erie, KS
316.244.3489

## Eisler Brothers Old Riverton Store (pg 118)
7109 SE Hwy 66 (Route 66)
Riverton, KS
620.848.3330

## Florence Deeble Rock Garden (pg 16)
Lucas, KS
Call Grassroots Arts Center for directions, 785.525.6118

## Garden of Eden (pgs 13-15)
305 E 2nd St
Lucas, KS
785.525.6395

## Grassroots Art Center (pgs 17-18)
213 S Main St
Lucas, KS
785.525.6118
http://grassrootsart.home.att.net/

## Henry's Sculpture Hill (bonus)
North side of Hwy 54,
East of Augusta, KS
Sculptures with literary themes.
Call for a tour.
620.321.9333

## Hubbell's Rubble (bonus)
Hwy 99
Howard, KS
Big yard of junk sculptures.

## M.T. Liggett (pgs 18-19)
Along Hwy 154
West of Mullinville, KS

## Ray O Smith (pgs 8-9) (Giant Concretealo)
Longford, KS
Call Grassroots Arts Center for directions, 785.525.6118

## Rock City (bonus)
3.5 miles south on SR 106,
Minneapolis, KS
Sandstone concretions (aka rocks) left behind prior to the Ice Age. We think they have other prehistoric origins, left behind by the dinosaurs.

## Tallgrass Prairie National Preserve (bonus)
Hwy 177
Between Cottonwood Falls, KS and Strong City, KS

## Vera's Tavern (pg 12)
Hunter, KS
The Tavern is one of 5 buildings in Hunter. It is is no longer operated by Vera.

## World's Largest Ball of Twine (pgs 10-11)
U.S. Hwy 24
Cawker City, KS

## World's Largest Hand-dug Well and the Pallasite Meteorite (bonus)
315 S. Sycamore
Greensburg, KS
Walk down the 105 stairs and back up the 105 stairs!

# KENTUCKY

## Wigwam Village Motel (pg 40)
601 N Dixie Hwy
Cave City, KY
270.773.3381

# LOUISIANA

## Big Al Taplet's Shoe Shine Parlor (pg 156-157)
1338 St. Bernard Street
New Orleans, LA
Or catch him on Jackson Square in the French Quarter.

**Dr. Bob (pgs 154-155)**
3027 Chartres
New Orleans, LA
www.drbobart.com

**Kenny Hill's Garden of Salvation (pgs 148-151)**
Bayouside Drive
Chavin, LA
Along the Bayou Petit Caillou

**UCM Museum (pgs 152-153)**
22275 Hwy 36
Abita Springs, LA
985.892.2624

## MICHIGAN

**Disneyland North (pg 86-87)**
12087 Klinger
Hamtramck, MI

**Heidelberg Project (pgs 82-83)**
Detroit, MI
From I-75, take the #51B exit. Merge onto Gratiot Ave./M-3. Turn slight right onto Heidelberg Street. Can be viewed from street
313. 537.8037
www.heidelberg.org

**Silvio's Italian-American Museum & Pizzeria (pg 84-85)**
26417 Plymouth Road
Redford, MI (suburb of Detroit)
313.937.2288

**Traveler's Club Restaurant and Tuba Museum (bonus)**
2138 Hamilton
Okemos, MI
Great food, microbrews and big horns.
517.349.1701

## MISSISSIPPI

**Attic Gallery (pg 161)**
1101 Washington Street
Vicksburg, MS
601.638.9221

**Bette Mott (pg 160)**
601 West Georgia Ave
McComb, MS
601.684.9636

**Earl Simmons' Gallery of Art (pg 161)**
6444 Warriors Trail
Vicksburg, MS
601.638.4635

**L.V. Hull (The Shoe Lady) (pg 166)**
123 Allen Street
Kosciusko, MS

**Margaret's Grocery (pgs 162-163)**
4535 North Washington St.
(Old Hwy 61)
Vicksburg, MS

**Walter Anderson Museum (pgs 158-159)**
510 Washington Ave.
Ocean Springs, MS
228.872.3164
www.walterandersonmuseum.org

## MISSOURI

**Black Madonna Shrine & Grottos (pg 33)**
St. Joseph Road
Eureka, MO
314.938.5361
www.blackmadonnashrine.org

**Cathedral of the Prince of Peace World's Smallest Church (pg 124)**
405 Kentling Ave
Highlandville, MO
417.443.3951

**City Museum, including the Museum of Mirth, Mystery and Mayhem.(pgs 34-36)**
701 N 15th St
St Louis, MO
314.231.2489

**Elvis Is Alive Museum (pgs 31-32)**
I-70 Frontage Road
Wright City, MO
314.745.3154

**Hammer Shed (pg 20)**
405 Elmwood Box 163
Norborne, MO

**J.C. Carter (bonus)**
21 Ne 600th Rd (off Hwy 13)
Warrensburg, MO
Metalwork and singing dogs.
Call for appointment.
660.747.5506

**Jim the Wonder Dog Park (pgs 42-43)**
North Lafayette Street
Marshall, MO
www.jimthewonderdog.com

**Lambert's Cafe (bonus)**
2515 East Malone
Sikeston, MO
Home of Throwed Rolls
314.471.4261

**Larry Baggett's Trail of Tears Monument (pgs 29-30)**
21250 State Rt D
Newburg, MO
It can be seen from I-44
1 mile west of Jerome, MO

**Old Drum Statue (bonus)**
On the courthouse square.
Warrensburg, MO
A tribute to the dog that inspired "Man's Best Friend" speech.

**Onyx Mountain Cavern (pg 29)**
Off I-44, at exit 172
Newburg, MO
573.762.3341

**Ralph Lanning Sculpture Park (pg 126)**
7295 West Farm Rd 170
Republic, MO
Junction of Hwy 60 & Hwy M/MM

**Rhett and Kelly Johnson (bonus)**
Route Z,
Dearborn, MO
Salvaged metal sculpture and bead work. Call for an appointment.
816.450.3616

**Robert E. Smith (pgs 122-124)**
Springfield, MO
His work is not open to the public, but can be seen throughout town.

**The Wheel Drive-In (pgs 26-27)**
Junction of US 50 & US 65
Sedalia, MO
660.826.5177

## MONTANA

**Charles Ringer Gallery (bonus)**
Hwy 212
Joliet, MT
Cool kinetic sculptures.
406.962.3705

**The Jersey Lilly (pg 94)**
1st And Main
Ingomar, MT
406.358.2278

**Paris Gibson Square Museum of Art (pg 91)**
1400 1st Ave. N.
Great Falls, MT
406.727.8255

**Tim Anderson's Little Mansion (pg. 92)**
Roundup, MT

## NEBRASKA

**Carhenge (pgs 100-101)**
Just north of Hwy 385
Alliance, NE

**Loi Vo's Bumper Art (pgs 96-97, 100)**
11400 SW 27th Street
Lincoln, NE
Private property. Please view from the street.

**Ole's Big Game Steakhouse (pg 100)**
113 N Oak St
Paxton, NE
308.239.4500

**Richard Martin's Yard (pg 99)**
708 Prentiss St
Mason City, NE
308.732.3458

**World's Largest Time Capsule (pg 98)**
Seward, NE
Next to House of Davisson Furniture.
Contact Seward Visitors Center,
402.643.4189

## NEW MEXICO

**Rancho Bonito (pg 111)**
901 US Hwy 60
Mountainair, NM
505.847.2577

**Tinkertown (pg 108)**
Sandia Park, NM
505.281.523
www.tinkertown.com

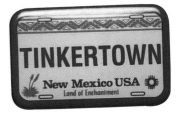

## NORTH DAKOTA

**Enchanted Highway (pg 95)**
Between Gladstone & Regent, ND
County Market Road off of I-94 (take Exit 72 south).

## OKLAHOMA

**Blue Whale (pg. 114)**
Old Route 66
Catoosa, OK

**Tom Mix Museum (bonus)**
721 N. Delaware
Dewey, OK
Contains the infamous
"Suitcase of Death."
918.534.1555

**Tool Fence (pg. 116)**
11448 East 163rd N
Collinsville, OK
Can be viewed from the road

**Totem Pole Park (pg 117)**
Foyil, OK
4 miles E on SH-28A
918.342.9149

## SOUTH DAKOTA

**Corn Palace (pgs 62-63)**
604 N Main St
Mitchell, SD
605.996.7311

## TENNESSEE

**JL Nippers (pg 41)**
Beech Grove, TN

**Memorial Park Cemetery (bonus)**
5668 Poplar Ave.
Memphis, TN
Another *rustico naturale* sculptural
environment by Dionicio Rodriguez.

## TEXAS

**Beer Can House (pg 141)**
222 Malone
Houston, TX
Contact Orange Show Foundation for
more info, 713.926.6368

**Dan Blocker Gravesite (pg 142)**
DeKalb Cemetery
DeKalb, TX

**Eyes of the World (pg 146)**
Inside the J & J Steakhouse
6685 Eastex Freeway
Beaumont, TX
409.860.3310

**Flower Man (pg 140)**
3317 Sampson
Houston, TX
His art is visible from the street.
Contact Orange Show Foundation for
more info, 713.926.6368

**The Orange Show (pgs 138-189)**
2402 Munger St.
Houston, TX
713.926.6368
www.insync.net/orange

**Texas Sacred Gardens (pg 136)**
Sam Houston National Forest
394 FM Road 1375 West
New Waverly, TX
936.344.6205

**Vince Hanneman's Cathedral
(bonus)**
4422 Lareina Drive
Austin, TX
Incredible 3-story backyard
environment.
512.442.3612

**X-Meah (pg 147)**
The Art Museum of Southeast Texas
500 Main Street
Beaumont, TX
Contains some of his works in
permanent collection.
409.832.3432
www.xmeah.com

## WISCONSIN

**Dickeyville Grotto (pgs 56-57)**
Holy Ghost Church
305 W Main
Dickeyville, WI
608.568.3119 or 608.568.7519

**Forevertron (pgs 64, 66-67)**
Baraboo, WI
Behind Delaney's Surplus Yard
Along Highway 12, five miles
south of Baraboo.

**Fred Smith's Wisconsin Concrete Park (pgs 70-71)**
N8236 State Highway 13
Phillips, WI
715.339.6475

**Nick Engelbart's Grandview (pg 50)**
Highway 39
West of Hollandale, WI

**Jurustic Park (pgs 76-77)**
M222 Sugarbush Lane
Marshfield, WI
Reservations are required.
715.387.1653

**Kohler Art Center (pgs 78-79)**
608 New York Avenue
Sheboygan, WI
920.458.6144
www.jmkac.org

**LaReau's World of Minatures (bonus)**
N6668 Hwy 22
Pardeeville, WI
Utter styrofoam madness.
608.429.3529

**Mt. Horeb Mustard Museum (pg 51)**
109 East Main Street
Mt. Horeb, WI
608.437.3986

**Norske Nook Restaurant and Bakery (bonus)**
Osseo, Rice Lake & Hayward, WI
Best darn pies in the world!

**Paul Hefti's Bottle Yard (pgs 58, 60)**
515 Adams Street
LaCrosse, WI
Private property. Please view from the street.

**Prairie Moon Sculpture Park (pg 55)**
Off Hwy 35
Between Fountain City
& Cochrane, WI

**Rock In The House (pg 54)**
Hwy 35
Fountain City, WI
North edge of town, look for the sign.

**Rudolph Grotto Gardens & Wonder Cave (pgs 68-69)**
6957 Grotto Ave.
Rudolph, WI
715.435.3120 or 435.3774

**Rudy Rotter Sculpture Museum (pgs 74-75)**
701 Buffalo Street
Manitowoc, WI
Hours by appointment only
920.682.6671
www.rudyrotter.com

**Tony's Fan Fair (pg 72)**
556 West Harding Ave.
Stevens Point, WI
Private property. Please view from the street.

**Wegner Grotto (pg 61)**
State Hwy 71
Cataract, WI
Many of the sculptures are covered during the winter. Call for tour information
608.269.8680

Don's not the only one who has donned "camera guy" gear to capture the images of these amazing sites. Thanks to the following people who contributed their photography for the making of this book:

Bill Christman (pg 38)
Ted Degener (pg 167)
Grassroots Art Center (pgs 9, 16)
Richard Gwinn (pgs 112-113)
Larry Harris (pgs 10, 16, 48-50, 54-55, 59-61, 65-66, 79, 117, 137-138, 140-141, 174-175, 183, front cover)
Don Ludwig (pg 112)
Kelly Ludwig (pgs i, 8-12, 14-19, 29-32, 36-38, 119, front and back covers)
Mt. Horeb Mustard Museum (pg 51)
Paris Gibson Square Museum of Art (pg 91)
Tony Perniciaro (pg 102)
Mark J. Ratledge (pg 90)
Mike Robins (pg 28)
Arlene Segal (pgs 6, 7)
Dan Slaughter (pg 53)
Bill Swislow (pgs 70-71, 167, 176-177)
Lyle Alan White (pg 18 - Inez's Photo)
Sandy Woodson (pgs 20-21, 31-35)

Additional Photos Provided By:
Randy Mason, Mike Murphy,
Don "The Camera Guy" Mayberger

Maps Illustrated by Gentry Mullins.

# Index

# "AND THAT GIANT BALL OF TAPE IS A WORLD RECORD HOLDER"

Our strong, silent companion dates back to 1982, inspired by Cawker City's Big Ball of Twine. Don and I had gone there to shoot the city's annual "Twine-a-thon". We sold some of the footage to "Ripley's Believe It or Not" and came away determined to make a "World's Largest" of our own.

But we needed something that challengers would be unlikely to use. So we settled on videotape, which was plentiful in the workplace. We wound until it hurt. All tape, no cereal-filler. Then we took pictures, congratulated ourselves and got rejected by David Letterman twice. So the ball sat in my garage until 1995, when someone had the bright idea to take it with us on the road to "announce our intentions." It worked, amazingly well.

And whenever people asked, "Is it *really* the world's largest?" we'd reply, "Have you seen a bigger one?" Finally, last year someone said, "Yes."

John Maas, an eigth-grade teacher at Holy Cross Luthern School, had built a ball of his own, shamelessly using student labor in the name of "science." The class challenged us, and sad to say, pretty much whupped us in every category.

But TV Weasels don't take defeat easily. We sent Don home to wind (and wind) some more, until those pesky eighth-graders would cry "uncle." We've weighed again (53 pounds now!) and though it's virtually a dead heat, I still say ours is the biggest. If John doesn't like it, HE CAN GET HIS OWN SHOW.

Happy trails.                    — RM

Original art by Jackie Denning

## MORE SCHOLARLY THAN US!

*P*eople ask us many things. "Down the hall, and to the left," is usually the answer. Another question is "where do you find all this stuff?" While there's no single all-encompassing source, there are plenty of good research tools out there for would-be road trippers. On the web, there's Roadside America (www.roadsideamerica.com), which does a great job of tracking the odd and unusual. For those more intrigued by art and artists, Chicago's Intuit (www.outsider.art.org) and Bill Swislow's site (www.interestingideas.com) are fine ways to further your knowledge.

And since you've already bought THIS book (good choice, I might add) here are some others we've found that might help you. To contact us or order tapes of the show, visit our site at

**www.kcpt.org/rare_visions**

**Sacred Spaces & Other Places: A Guide to Grottos & Sculptural Environments in the Upper Midwest**
By Lisa Stone and Jim Zanzi
School of the Art Institute of Chicago

**Backyard Visionaries: Grassroots Art in the Midwest**
By Cathy Dwigans and Barbara Brackman
University Press of Kansas

**Self-Made Worlds: Visionary Folk Art Environments**
By Roger Manley and Mark Sloan
Aperture

**Gardens of Revelation: Environments by Visionary Artists**
By John Beardsley
Abbeville Press

**Fantasy Worlds**
By Deidi von Schaewen and John Maizels
Taschen

**Raw Creation: Outsider Art and Beyond**
By John Maizels
Phaidon Press Limited

**20th Century American Folk, Self Taught, and Outsider Art**
By Betty-Carol Sellen with Cynthia J. Johanson
Neal-Schuman Publishers, Inc.

**Little Museums: Over 1,000 Small (and Not-So-Small)**
**American Showplaces**
By Lynne Arany and Archie Hobson
Henry Holt and Company, Inc.

**Outsider Art of the South**
By Kathy Moses
Schiffer Publishing, LTD

**The Pioneer Spirit**
By Lyle Alan White
Walter Publications/The Lowell Press

**Home Away From Home: Motels in America**
By John Margolies
Bulfinch Press

**Soul in the Stone: Cemetery Art from the Heartland**
By John Gary Brown
University Press of Kansas

Musical contributors — The Plaid Family